LET THEM LEAD

Books by John U. Bacon

Blue Ice

America's Corner Store

Cirque Du Soleil: The Spark

Bo's Lasting Lessons

Three and Out

Fourth and Long

Endzone

Overtime

Playing Hurt by John Saunders
(with John U. Bacon)

The Great Halifax Explosion

The Best of Bacon

LET THEM
LEAD

Unexpected Lessons in Leadership
from America's Worst
High School Hockey Team

JOHN U. BACON

Houghton Mifflin Harcourt
Boston   New York
2021

For information about permission to reproduce selections from this book,
write to trade.permissions@hmhco.com or to Permissions,
Houghton Mifflin Harcourt Publishing Company, 3 Park Avenue,
19th Floor, New York, New York 10016.

hmhbooks.com

Library of Congress Cataloging-in-Publication Data
Names: Bacon, John U., 1964– author.
Title: Let them lead : unexpected lessons in leadership from America's
worst high school hockey team / John U. Bacon.
Description: Boston : Houghton Mifflin Harcourt, 2021. | Includes index.
Identifiers: LCCN 2021004077 (print) | LCCN 2021004078 (ebook) |
ISBN 9780358533269 (hardcover) | ISBN 9780358581741 (CD) |
ISBN 9780358581918 (audio) | ISBN 9780358540212 (ebook)
Subjects: LCSH: Leadership — Case studies. | Management — Case studies. |
Hockey teams — Michigan — Ann Arbor — Case studies.
Classification: LCC HD57.7 .B3228 2021 (print) | LCC HD57.7 (ebook) |
DDC 658.4/092—dc23
LC record available at https://lccn.loc.gov/2021004077
LC ebook record available at https://lccn.loc.gov/2021004078

Book design by Chrissy Kurpeski

Printed in the United States of America
1 2021
4500831217

To the players, the parents, and the assistant coaches,
who created an experience worth writing about,
and especially to Mike "Lapper" Lapprich,
the heart and soul of our team

Contents

Third Year Giving Control

Author's Note

This book is ostensibly about a high school boys' ice hockey team, but it's really about how to help men and women of all ages and backgrounds reach their potential.

My advice is simple: you have to create high expectations immediately, establish deep mutual trust, and then help your people take over. To do all that, you need to give them a ton of encouragement, reward their achievements — great and small — and then give them the power to run the show.

Is it easy? No. This approach requires a lot from them, and even more from you — including personal courage. But I'm convinced this is the best way to motivate today's workers — and once everyone's pulling in the same direction, the rewards are endless.

This is not to say you're reading a book by a know-it-all. Far from it. You'll see that, when I was hired to turn around Ann Arbor Huron High School's hockey team, I had a strong vision for what I wanted the team to become, but not much else. I didn't have shelves stacked with the latest business books or a binder full of strategies, tactics, and proven theories for rebuilding the program. Instead, often after my attempts to solve a stubborn problem had failed, I got a lot of ideas from my mentors, my colleagues, and my players, or I simply came up with something I figured was worth trying. We didn't turn it around through some grand strategy, but through trial and error.

I know these ideas work, because I've tried them.

I've coached eighteen seasons of high school soccer, baseball, and hockey, including the only coed squad in our high school's all-boys intramural softball league (we finished second of eleven teams); the University of Michigan women's ice hockey team; and the Ann Arbor Huron High School River Rats, the subject of this book. I've spent twenty of my last thirty-five years teaching in private and public high schools, community colleges, and Miami (Ohio) University, Northwestern University, and the University of Michigan, where the students awarded me the Golden Apple for "excellence in teaching." I've worked as a corporate trainer for Ford, Chrysler, and Subaru, and for the past decade, through speaking and consulting, I've helped organizations around the country excel. I now work part-time for Insight Global, a $2.5 billion company with offices in sixty-two North American cities and a staff that is 70 percent women.

So don't be fooled: this book isn't about high school hockey any more than the movie *Rocky* is about boxing or *Star Wars* is about outer space. You don't need to know anything about sports to follow the lessons here.

While this book does not claim to be a manual on diversity, equity, and inclusion, the ideas, policies, and practices offered here will be of direct help with these vital issues, particularly the chapters on hiring and the importance of being fair, giving everyone a chance, and listening to your people's problems. All are essential to leading a diverse, inclusive team on which everyone feels respected and valued.

Likewise, although most of this story takes place years before Covid-19 hit our shores — prompting millions of people to work remotely — the pandemic has made the principles presented here more pertinent than ever. One of our team's foundational beliefs applies here: "Your character is what you do when you think no one is watching." Since most managers can rarely watch their employees work these days, they need to be able to count on their people. This book will help you create an enduring culture of trust.

The best proof comes from our players themselves. When I started writing this book in 2020, I scoured the four thousand pages of notes I'd kept in fourteen computer journals and drew information from seven boxes filled with game files, statistics, programs, letters, and even videotapes. Those resources have allowed me to accurately recount more quotes, scenes, and stories than you'd expect in a retrospective. Any mistakes are naturally mine alone.

But one of the special features of this book, I believe, emerged only after I sent my former players and assistant coaches their passages — to confirm or correct them — a couple months before my deadline. I was asking them to do what we'd already done on the ice years before: work together to create the best possible results. Once again, they greatly exceeded my expectations, sending back 150 pages of stories, memories, and insights that only they could have provided. Countless times they told me things I had remembered differently, hadn't remembered at all, or could never have known. To say I was pleasantly surprised by their contributions is to understate the case considerably.

They even threw in a bonus: because they are now in their midthirties, they were able to describe how their experiences on our team had shaped their lives since. I believe you'll find this aspect of the book especially valuable, because the vast majority of the fifty-four players I coached are now leaders themselves, responsible for dozens and sometimes hundreds of people, in an amazing array of fields. Their positions include vice president of an engineering firm, executive chef of the University of Michigan's Residential Dining Division, public affairs adviser for cybersecurity and infrastructure at the Department of Homeland Security, junior high school social studies teacher, and general manager at Uber Freight, as well as plenty of doctors, lawyers, and managers.

In fact, these days I'm working for one of my previous captains, Stevie Wasik, now a vice president at the aforementioned Insight Global, the national staffing company based in Atlanta. Stevie recently started the company's Compass Division, teaching leadership and culture to Fortune 500 companies, using many of the principles he learned in the Huron hockey program. That's right. I work for a guy I first met when he was just a fourteen-year-old kid who came up to my elbow — and nothing could make me happier.

Most of my players are now married with kids, so they're coaching their sons' and daughters' hockey teams. Because I became a husband at forty-nine and a father at fifty-one, many of their kids are the same age as our five-year-old son Teddy, or older. When my former players come over for our annual barbecue, they bring their wives and kids, we set up play dates, and they give me parenting advice — and I have to take it.

They've seen enough of the world to know what works and what doesn't. I'm confident you'll agree that their voices add immeasurably to this story — a feature I believe is unique to this book.

Just as the unexpected success of our team belongs to the players and the assistant coaches, I owe this book to their good work too.

You guys are the best. Once again, *thank you.*

John U. Bacon
Fall 2020

Introduction

I give dozens of speeches every year to managers across the country about leadership, innovation, and diversity, among other top-
ics. The audiences have responded enthusiastically, for which I'm
grateful.

But these days there's always a kicker. As soon as I leave the stage
— or when I invite my virtual audience to ask questions — a few folks
inevitably approach me to discuss the speech. It's all very positive
until one of them delivers some version of a common complaint:
"My employees just don't 'get it' — or I just don't get them."

I've heard this so many times — from both men and women,
from rookie managers to senior supervisors and all levels of leadership in between, and from people in just about every industry you
can name — that I've concluded this must be a national epidemic.
Across the country managers are pulling their hair out trying to motivate their employees.

Once one of them breaks the ice, everyone starts chiming in.
The litany of complaints includes starkly different views of everything from proper communications and reasonable expectations
down to punctuality and even punctuation. Everyone nods, laughs,

or shakes their heads, until someone circles back to the main issue: "I feel like I don't understand them, or they don't understand me — or maybe both."

You probably already know how rapidly these issues can multiply when so many employees are working remotely from home. The distance between leaders and their people is growing, not shrinking. How can you monitor your employees' effort? How can you determine how well they're collaborating with their coworkers and clients? And how can you possibly instill your organization's culture when you almost never see your people in person? The Covid-19 pandemic, the turbulent economy, and everything that has followed are making leading effectively more complicated than ever — and more *important*.

The only thing that confounds these supervisors more than trying to manage their people is trying to sort through all the guidance they get from books, consultants, their bosses, and Human Resources on how to handle their people. There is no shortage of advice, of course — which is no surprise when you learn that teaching leadership to corporations is a $368 billion industry. (Yes, that's "*billions*," with a "b.") But there aren't many books about motivating the modern worker — and the advice offered by those that do cover it rarely works and often makes the situation worse.

"They tell us we have to cater to their every whim," one fed-up division head told me. "We're supposed to give them casual Fridays and 'Taco Tuesdays,' beanbag chairs and kombucha machines, just to get an honest day's work done."

I listen to their protests and stories without interrupting. I always get the feeling they've been dying to vent to someone outside their office who won't get them in trouble. But when I hear all this, I wonder: Have the experts who give all this advice ever actually *led* anyone? And if they have, does any of that stuff work? I honestly don't see how it could.

When my audience members have exhausted their problems and questions, I tell them, "I understand. I know what you're going through. I've been there, and I've done that — many times. But I think I can help you.

"Let me tell you a story — a true story."

A few years ago I took over the ice hockey team at my alma mater, Ann Arbor Huron High School, home of the River Rats (and no, I'm not making that name up).

The River Rats had just finished the previous season with a 0-22-3 record. For you non-sports fans out there, the "0" is where the wins go, the "22" indicates losses, and the "3" represents tie games. Everyone was so mad at everyone else — the players, the parents, the coaches, and even the administrators — that on the night of the team banquet the head coach stayed home, without telling anyone.

When I got the job, over the objections of some of the team's parents and players, I had never been a head hockey coach before. I also just happened to be the worst player in school history. So that meant the nation's worst team would be led by its worst former player — not exactly a combination that portended greatness.

Let Them Lead tells the story of how we worked together to change the way we thought, acted, dressed, worked, and performed — in that order. We created a "Huron Hockey Way" of doing just about everything, from working out to taping our socks to being on time for every team function — *always*. We often said, "Three o'clock means three o'clock," because we knew if we couldn't show up on time, ready to work, we certainly weren't going to be able to handle the complicated strategies hockey players must master to be successful.

But my approach wasn't "command-and-control," or "my way or the highway" stuff. I constantly solicited input from the assistant coaches and the players and engaged in a lot of give-and-take. Our ultimate goal was simple, if ambitious: we wanted the *players*, not the coaches, to run the team — *and they did*.

To that end, we had only two rules: work hard, and support your teammates. If they did those two things, even when we were getting blown out 13–2, I was satisfied, even proud, and I kept encouraging them. If they didn't do those two things, even when we were pummeling a lesser opponent, I was not happy — and they knew we'd be fixing those things as soon as the game ended.

My promise to them was straightforward: "I work hard for you. You work hard for me."

That must have hit home, because I heard them repeat it a thousand times. I meant every word and proved it to them every chance I had. In return, they more than kept up their end of the bargain, working harder than I ever imagined high school students could work. And let me tell you: they were something to see.

Our first year we finished with seven wins, the most improved team in school history. The next year we broke *that* record by adding nine more wins to finish with a record of 16-9-2, while also notching the state's highest team grade point average, a 3.27. For our third season together I set up a brutal schedule, with two-thirds of our games against top ten teams. But that didn't stop the River Rats from achieving a sterling 17-4-5 mark, the best record in school history.

To do all this, we didn't cut any players from the 0-22-3 team, recruit a roster of ringers, or make any deals with the devil. Everything they won, they earned.

We rose to number four in the state, and fifty-third nationally — thereby passing 940 of the nation's teams, or 95 percent, in just three years. More important were the values we learned and the strong sense of belonging that grew from pursuing a shared vision.

Make no mistake — the players are the heroes of this story. The long list includes my first captain, Mike Henry, who, after some early conflicts, realized he had the leadership potential to help turn the team around, and did so; Jon "Elmo" Eldredge, our first team's best player, also our funniest and most beloved, who was searching for his place on the team before becoming the conscience of the squad; Scott "Scooter" McConnell, our "Rudy," who scored his first and only goal with 3.3 seconds left in his last game; Rob DeMuro, who lost ninety pounds in one year and earned All-State Honorable Mention; and our revered assistant coach, nineteen-year-old Mike Lapprich, whom the players picked to win the team's Unsung Hero Award, though it had always gone to a player. They loved him that much.

Looking back, leading the Rats was the most consuming job I've ever had, but also the most rewarding. I'm still in touch with the players. I go to their weddings, and they come to my annual barbecue for the players, parents, and coaches of those teams — almost two decades after they played.

Motivating your team to lead themselves demands that you lead differently. This approach is not easier than the traditional approach, but it is more effective, and you'll be amazed by what your people can do. The fundamental principles we followed in the locker room will work just as well in the classroom or the conference room and get you the kind of results that conventional wisdom will not.

Along the way I've learned a few things, often the hard way, that can help you bring out the best in your people without making the same mistakes I did. Everything I'm going to tell you is simple, but none of it is easy, including:

- How to make your place special — by making it *hard.*
- How to get more by expecting more. You don't lower the bar, you *raise it.*
- Why you should be patient with your team's performance, but not their behavior.
- How to hire better and fire less by giving the bad news first.
- Why you should be the *dumbest* person on your staff.

- Why you need to get to know your people and have fun while you're working.

- How to teach people to set goals *they* want to achieve.

- How to make team members accountable *to each other*.

- Why you can't play favorites, or take credit for their success.

- Why you should strive to be replaced — and the sooner the better.

I'll tell you stories from coaching the River Rats that taught me each lesson — lessons that work just about anywhere, from high school hockey teams to Fortune 500 companies. You'll see why this advice will help you succeed where many have failed, and keep you happy while you're doing it.

Yes, I've heard today's workers are lazy, sloppy, and selfish. But I'm here to tell you:

They *want* discipline.
They *want* direction.
They *want* to be challenged.
They *want* to lead.

They want work that offers more than money and titles. They want to be part of something bigger than themselves, because they crave *meaning, purpose,* and *belonging*. Providing all that is admittedly hard work — but it's more than worth it.

The story you're about to read is not so much about coaching a high school hockey team as it is about leading people: what they really want, how to give it to them, and why they will give you everything you could ever ask for in return, and then some.

If it worked for America's worst high school hockey team, it can work anywhere.

Changing the Culture

1

When You're on the Floor, You Can't Fall out of Bed

- Get all the help you can. No one can do this alone.

- Don't try to fool your people. They'll soon know you better than you know yourself.

- To make it *special* to be on your team, make it *hard* to be on your team.

When I applied to coach my high school alma mater's ice hockey team, the Ann Arbor Huron High School River Rats, I had already heard all the warnings about the upcoming generation in general, and these guys in particular.

Those who had seen them play told me the players were not merely an unskilled, uninspired group, but one of the worst teams ever assembled. They had finished the previous season with a record of 0-22-3, and had not won a single contest in more than a year.

Starting the next year, my first as head coach, US High School Hockey Online (USHSHO.com) ranked every high school hockey team in the nation, so there were no rankings for Huron's infamous 0-22-3 record the previous season. But since USHSHO.com had ranked a high school team in Madison, New Jersey, dead last in 2000–2001 with a 4-10-2 record, and ranked Twinsburg, Ohio, last the next two years with identical 0-22 records, it seems safe to assume that Huron's 0-22-3 record would have earned the River Rats the dubious distinction of being the worst team in America that year. They might have been ranked last the year before that too, when they finished 3-20-3.

Impressive, in a way.

The River Rats were so bad that the athletic director, many of the parents, and even some of the players wanted to drop out of the Michigan Metro Hockey League, the state's best circuit – provided the league didn't drop the River Rats first. The Metro League's dozen teams – hailing from Detroit's white-collar suburbs and from "downriver," Detroit's blue-collar suburbs, plus the two Ann Arbor high schools, Huron and Pioneer, our archrival – had already produced thirty-one state champions in all three divisions, dwarfing the twenty-two for the rest of the state combined.

The River Rats had been playing in the Metro League since the school started in 1967–1968, but in the two seasons before I applied for the position, the Rats hadn't won a single Metro League game. In the previous three years, they hadn't beaten crosstown rival Pioneer either, and they played them at least twice a year. Some parents were even talking about demoting the team, the school's most expensive sport, from varsity to club status – a move I felt would essentially kill the program. In any event, if the team didn't drop out of the league, get kicked out, or fold altogether, a lot of the current players planned on quitting the team, and maybe the sport, anyway.

The River Rats seemed to have every problem in the book: untalented and unmotivated, they wore their failure with a kind of perverse pride, like a badge of honor. They even made shirts featuring their abysmal record – "0-20" at the time – and wore them to the school dance, where they gathered in the center of the room to chant "0 and 20!" to their mystified classmates.

The team's 0-22-3 finish was only the latest in a series of denouements for Huron's hockey coaches. All three of my predecessors had enjoyed early success, coached ten or eleven years, then finished with their worst seasons, establishing Huron as the graveyard of hockey coaches. When I met with the team's previous coach, whom I had assisted for four years earlier in the decade, he told me he knew the players had held meetings behind his back. The parents had too.

And yet I still wanted the job. After I had applied, I met with our venerable trainer, Rod Sorge (rhymes with "corgi," with a hard "g"), who looks like Peter Sellers's Inspector Clouseau. He had been on staff when I played twenty years earlier. He pulled me into his school office, a windowless concrete bunker about the size of a walk-in closet, to lay it on the line.

"It got so bad last year," Sorge told me, "that some of the parents demanded the athletic director fire the coach. When she refused, I heard some parents planned to corner him at the team banquet and force him to resign on the spot."

That got my attention.

"But when the coach caught wind of their scheme," Sorge continued, "he outsmarted them, if you will, by not showing up at the season-ending banquet at all. He didn't tell anyone about his plan, not even me."

As the minutes passed at the banquet, with the players and parents staring down at their cold food, people slowly realized the coach wasn't coming. The reactions ranged from confusion to relief to anger to sadness. Scott "Scooter" McConnell recalls that the athletic director finally went to the podium and said, "'By now, you've probably noticed someone is missing. Coach has submitted his letter of resignation.' At some point she got choked up and said, 'I'm sorry. I think he's a good person and this is hard.'"

That strikes me as fair: he was an old-school coach whose teams hadn't won many games, but he was a fundamentally decent person.

The athletic director then explained the process for selecting a new coach, right there at the banquet, and took questions. When some of the parents suggested that Huron drop out of the Metro League, she said there were no good options except to play as an independent team, but they could discuss that later.

"What a mess," Sorge recalled, shaking his head. "After twenty-five years working with hundreds of teams, I thought I'd seen everything. But I'd never seen that."

If the job posting wasn't very appealing for the average businessperson, teacher, or coach, it should have been less so for me. I had been a sportswriter with the *Detroit News* writing Sunday feature stories, a dream job I threw my heart into, often pulling all-nighters to finish stories. But even with the long hours and travel, I still woke up early twice a week to teach an adult hockey class at 7:30 a.m., and assisted the University of Michigan women's hockey team at night. I had not shaken the coaching bug, which first bit me when I was a nineteen-year-old college kid coaching a team of ninth-grade baseball players.

I left the *Detroit News* when I realized that, while I was writing about great leaders and great teams, I was still an observer, not a participant. I'd meet the subjects of my story on Monday and say goodbye on Friday. Still single, my life felt like it was too much about me. As the old Yes song goes, "Don't surround yourself with yourself."

I wanted to build something with others, something that felt like family, something that could last.

I was now trying to make my living as a freelance writer. That required even longer hours, lots of travel, and great flexibility, none of which jibed with daily hockey workout and practice times, twenty-five games on Wednesday and Saturday nights, and the extensive off-season work necessary to turn around this particular team.

My attraction to coaching certainly wasn't the money, since the position paid a grand total of $5,000 for the four-month season, and nothing for the off-season workouts, practices, and games. If there was any prestige that attached to coaching the nation's worst high school hockey team, it was hard to see.

Why did I think I could avoid the fate of Huron's previous coaches? Why did I even want to try?

Despite at least a dozen solid reasons *not* to apply for this job, I did want it – badly. But none of my reasons were tangible. It wasn't salary, status, or ambition. I never aspired to become a full-time coach like Jon Cooper, who coached Lansing Catholic Central at the same time I was applying for Huron's job and who would go on to lead the NHL's Tampa Bay Lightning to the Stanley Cup. I had no desire to coach anywhere else after Huron. I had daydreamed about coaching the River Rats for years.

Yes, I wanted to save the program from leaving the Metro League, being demoted to club status, or disbanding altogether. I wanted to turn the team around, notch some winning seasons, and prove to ourselves and the world that we weren't a pathetic pack of losers. But even those goals were not enough to motivate me to want the job.

I was not interested in leading a win-at-all-costs program. If that's all you're trying to do, what do you have when you lose? Nothing. I longed to create something deeper and more enduring.

I planned to be tough, leading a sharp, hardworking squad while instilling the highest standards of conduct on and off the ice. But I didn't want to be a dictator, merely trying to enforce my will on the players. I wanted the coaches and players to build something special *together* – a program that would be a source of pride for the school and the town, but especially for the players who created it. I didn't want them to feel they *had* to dress appropriately, work hard, and avoid stupid penalties. I wanted them to *want* to do those things, and to *feel good* about doing them as a statement of who they were.

I didn't want a locker room divided into cliques by age or status either, with the older "cool kids" taunting or ignoring the younger ones, which is too often what happens in high school locker rooms. No, I wanted every one of them to feel that, as soon as they opened the door to our locker room, they deserved to be there as much as anyone else, and that everyone within those walls had their back. They were safe, and they belonged.

Unlike the previous season, when the players avoided wearing any Huron hockey garb at school, around town, or even at our own arena — except for the handmade "0-and-20" T-shirts they wore to the school dance — I wanted them to walk through the hallways in new team T-shirts, sweats, and jerseys declaring who they were, and what they stood for, without irony, embarrassment, or apology, but with actual *pride.* I wanted them to get emotional at the senior banquet, fighting back tears while saying goodbye to an experience that had stamped them forever — and a program they would want to support long after they left.

If you had asked me to point to one metric or other that could confirm our success, a number that would prove we had arrived, as so many businesses require of their leaders, I couldn't have done it. There was simply no way I could calculate what the return on investment would be, or how long it would take for all this to gel. I could not tell you how many wins we'd need to get, or how many All-State players we'd need to produce, or how many rivals we'd need to beat, or how many weeks ranked in the top ten we'd need to notch before we could say we had achieved all this. Yes, I wanted those things, but I figured they were not the end itself, but would come as the by-products of a bigger mission.

Even if I couldn't give you numbers, I could have told you exactly how my dream program would look, and how it would *feel.* If I'd had to pick three words, they would have been *commitment, purpose,* and *belonging.* I wanted to be part of something they all wanted to be part of too — a team where everyone would be eager to make their contributions. I wanted everyone to feel that we were accomplishing something bigger than just winning games. I wanted to show the hockey world what a true team looked like every night, win or lose. And I wanted our locker room to be the center of our work, the headquarters, the fire in the middle of our base camp, a private sanctuary where everyone felt comfortable, welcome, and valued. With all these things going for us, I expected to be a team that overachieved, that punched above our weight class, that beat teams that should have trampled us, and tormented the rest. We would be something to see, on and off the ice.

In short, I wanted to lead a program I would have loved to have played for myself, one that could've provided memories and lessons I could have taken with me as a source of strength to draw on the rest of my life. That's what I wanted for them.

The rest was details.

Perhaps shockingly, Huron's coaching position attracted seven serious candidates. Apparently I was not alone in my desire to take my chances in the graveyard of coaches.

My candidacy had some pluses, a couple major minuses, and one ace.

After I earned my degree in history — or "pre-unemployment" — I turned down Albany Academy in New York and LaLumiere School in LaPorte, Indiana, to take a position that offered half the pay and status — such as they were — to become a "faculty intern" at Culver Academies in Indiana. I student-taught US history, coached JV soccer and baseball, and assisted their top hockey team, all for the princely salary of $9,000 — high four figures.

On paper my decision to pick Culver looked foolish, like so many of my career decisions. But it was worth it because of Culver's head hockey coach, Al Clark. In one season working for him, I learned most of what I needed to know to coach a high school hockey team.

Clark grew up playing hockey outdoors in Thunder Bay, Ontario, at the western tip of Lake Superior. At the University of New Hampshire (UNH) he captained the golf team twice and the hockey team once and earned Phi Beta Kappa as a math major. He would be inducted into the UNH Hall of Fame alongside NHL All-Star Rod Langway and baseball Hall of Fame catcher Carlton Fisk. When Clark had to decline an offer from the Toronto Maple Leafs because of his badly damaged shoulders, he earned his master's in mathematics instead.

When a Culver board member, Cummins Engine Company CEO Jim Henderson, wanted to start a hockey program to entice his teenage sons to attend his alma mater, UNH coach Charlie Holt told him, "I have your coach. Do not take no for an answer."

Good thing, because "no" is exactly what Clark told Henderson three times before he finally agreed to visit Culver's gorgeous campus. It worked. In 1976 Clark started the Culver Eagles' hockey program with some kids who had never skated before.

The Eagles' secret weapon was a coach who rarely smiled or even spoke, and never yelled or swore. Whether Clark's team was up by five goals or down by five, he looked like a man waiting for a bus in the rain. Emotional Al Clark is not, but he knew the game, how to teach it, and how to motivate his players — despite barely talking to them. It was years before I learned how he did it.

In only their third season, the Eagles won their first state title — then eight more before the state disallowed their A-team from competing. So Culver sent its B-team to win the Indiana state title, while Culver's A-team now battles AAA elite travel teams for the national title. When Clark stepped down in 2015, he had produced more than one hundred Division I college hockey players, twenty-five NHL draft picks, nine NHLers (including 1986 NHL Rookie of the Year Gary Suter), and five US Olympians, while winning 1,017 games, the most in the history of US high school hockey. Along the way Clark was named National Coach of the Year in 1994 and started Culver's girls' program in 1998. He turned down many college offers, because Culver was where he felt he belonged.

When I assisted Clark in 1986–1987, the team was loaded with future college players and two future NHLers. But what impressed me most was how Clark got his players to buy in. Early on, he offered his first tip to me: "Don't try to fool these guys. By the end of the season, they'll know you better than you know yourself."

He was right, of course. You can't fake authenticity — and teenagers have the most sensitive BS detectors around. Don't even try it.

. . .

Having Clark's support for the Huron High School job was my ace, but it was easily offset by two major minuses: I had never been a head hockey coach before, and even worse in the search committee's eyes, I'd served as an assistant coach for Huron's previous head coach five years earlier.

Finally, I just happened to be the worst player in Huron High School hockey history. This is not false modesty. I can prove this empirically. I still hold the record for the most games in a Huron uniform, eighty-six, with the fewest goals: *zero*.

It's actually a family record. My brother also played for Huron, and he also failed to score — though he likes to point out that he played goalie.

Hey, we've all got excuses.

Years later, in the senior leagues, I was a top-five scorer a couple of times, and at our annual Huron hockey alumni games I'm usually good for a goal or two and the occasional hat trick. In short, I got better — or, in the words of University of Michigan coach Red Berenson, I was a "late bloomer."

But beer league stats don't count for much, so I carried this checkered past into the interview room, where the search had boiled down to me and a candidate with more experience. We were interviewed in Sorge's classroom by a six-person committee consisting of Sorge; the athletic director, Jane Bennett, a kind woman who had been my eighth-grade algebra teacher; her assistant; two hockey parents; and one player, Mike Henry, the previous year's assistant captain, who'd been named the next team's incoming captain at the infamous banquet.

They sat in school desk chairs in a semicircle, with me sitting in the center, facing the firing squad. When they asked me what I planned to do, I was prepared with my notes, my theories, and my convictions. I responded confidently that I would run a no-nonsense program that would emphasize personal accountability, hard work, and teamwork. The whole point of a good high school hockey program, I added, was not to win college scholarships but to produce young men prepared to lead, despite whatever life might throw at them.

If they weren't too impressed by that, they liked my next answer even less.

"How do you plan to do that?" one of the parents asked.

"We will be the hardest-working high school hockey team in the state," I said. "We will start working out in the weight room on Monday, June 26 — one week after school gets out — to do baseline tests to see where we stand. I'll give them a plan to work out all summer, and we will have off-ice workouts before every practice."

I will never forget the cold silence that followed.

After the interviews were over, the hiring committee voted 4–2 — for the other guy. Only Sorge and the team parent who knew me, Steve Sheldon, had voted for me. The athletic director, her assistant, the other parent, and the incoming captain had all voted for the other candidate.

That would have been that, if Sorge and Steve Sheldon had not refused to concede. As Sorge recalls, "Steve and I were sure we needed a guy who first and foremost could get the players to buy in. We also thought that one of our own, a Huron alum, would have the best chance of doing that. We tried to convince the others that coaching philosophy, management style, X's and O's and the like, wouldn't mean squat if you couldn't win the players over."

During the deliberations that followed, Sorge turned his chair around so my two allies were sitting back to back, each trying to persuade two of the other committee members to change their vote. The other parent, the captain, and the assistant AD weren't budging, but when the athletic director finally flipped her vote, they had achieved a 3–3 split decision. The deadlock would be broken by the school principal, who knew little about me and less about hockey.

The next week I met with Sorge in his classroom before my interview with the principal. While Sorge walked with me to the principal's office at the far end of the school, he told me, "I really hope you don't get this job."

"Why?" I asked, stopping in my tracks. I was incredulous that my biggest backer would say this.

"Because I like you," Sorge said, "and you have no idea what you're in for."

After I finished the interview, I walked back to Sorge's office.

"Well?" he asked.

"I thought it went pretty well," I said, with cautious optimism.

"That's what you thought after you interviewed with the committee," Sorge said, reminding me that they had initially voted 4–2 for the other guy.

A few days later Sorge called. The urgency with which I picked up the phone surprised me. I wanted this job more than I had admitted to myself.

"I have bad news," he said in a flat voice.

My heart sank. "I didn't get it?"

"No," he said. "You did."

I brightened, then asked, "So, wait—what's the bad news?"

"That *is* the bad news."

Sorge meant that getting the job was bad news for me, but plenty of Huron's players and parents regarded my hiring as bad news for them too, and for the team.

"I vividly remember driving by Huron High School after the selection was announced," hockey mom Robin Kunkel told me. When she learned that the new coach, yours truly, was a thirty-five-year-old who had been an assistant for the previous head coach, she thought, *Really?! Why, why couldn't we get a real coach, someone older and really good, someone who had coached a winning hockey team? Couldn't the school do a more extensive search and hire someone who wasn't just an alum?*

Robin Kunkel was far from alone. I already knew that the search committee had first voted 4–2 for the other candidate, but I had no way of knowing the depth of the team's disappointment in my hiring. That was probably just as well.

When I stopped by my parents' house to tell them I'd just been hired to coach the 0-22-3 Huron hockey team, my father shrugged and said, "Well, when you're on the floor, you can't fall out of bed."

Thanks, Dad.

A few days later I met with Al Clark, who happened to be in Ann Arbor to conduct a tryout for a national all-star hockey team at our arena. On a beautiful June day we ate lunch at a sidewalk table downtown.

I confessed, "I feel like the dog chasing the car who actually catches it, but then realizes he lacks a driver's license, car keys, and opposable thumbs."

"Well, it's your team now," Clark said, in his trademark monotone.

What Clark had done at Culver was incredibly impressive; starting with an outdoor rink and a dozen kids who had never played the game before, he built them into perennial state champions, and a national power.

What I was attempting would be easier in many ways. We certainly weren't starting from scratch. Huron's program had been established more than three decades earlier; we practiced and played in a three-rink complex that was so nice the USA Hockey program ran its two national junior teams out of the building; and our players and parents were seasoned hockey families, familiar with the idiosyncrasies of a unique sport.

But if Clark's first bunch of players had been inexperienced and naive, they were still excited and optimistic about their new endeavor. Our players were jaded, cynical, and burnt out, ready to quit the team and maybe the sport. If Al's job was to teach his inexperienced players the game and create a winning culture, mine was to teach my people a new mindset and turn the culture of apathy around.

"So," I asked him, "what do I do?"

"The first thing you do," he said, "is to make it special to play for Huron."

"We're already the worst team in America," I said. "Isn't that special enough?"

Clark ignored my little joke. "And the best way to make it special," he continued, "is to make it *hard*."

Clark's advice was the exact opposite of what everyone else had been telling me: athletes, students, and employees have all changed; I shouldn't expect too much; and I have to accommodate *them*, not the other way around.

But Clark had a point. The Peace Corps accepts about one in six applicants. The Navy SEALS accept a mere 6 percent, and 75 percent of *those* drop out. How can they afford to be so picky? Those jobs don't pay much. A Peace Corps volunteer makes a few hundred dollars a month, while a typical SEAL makes about $54,000 a year. You don't get famous doing those jobs either. And the work is brutally hard. But the *hard part* is exactly why the right people want to see if they can hack it. They are not *repulsed* by the difficulty of those jobs. They're *attracted* to it.

If I had any regrets about telling the committee that we would be the hardest-working high school hockey team in the state, Clark's advice erased it.

But it's important to clarify that Clark's approach was not to be confused with a command-and-control dictatorship. I never saw Al take any pleasure in punishing his players. Everything he did, he did to make them better. He *wanted* them to succeed — *he was on their side* — and they felt that. He just didn't think his players or his team could get very far without being disciplined.

He elaborated (to the degree that he ever did): "You need to make players feel like they had to do something hard just to make the team — something not everyone would be willing to do — so they know just making the team means they accomplished something. And once that culture is established, it is relatively easy to maintain because the players, with a little guidance, will do it for you."

Ah. *There it was.* The answer to the mystery behind his incredible success. In just a few words, Clark had given me the first steps I'd be taking that season.

Al talked, while I scribbled notes. His message reminded me of something the best leaders I'd encountered in athletics, education, and business had all said, in one way or another: Your people will never *ask* for it, but down deep they *want* discipline. They *want* direction. They *want* to be challenged. They *want* to belong to something that's difficult to join.

"Do that," Al said, "and they will give you more than you could ever ask for."

The check came. I signed it, stood up, and shook Al's hand.

"I cannot thank you enough," I said.

He waved that off, and that's when I recognized the obvious: he was already coaching me, using the same principles he wanted me to use — and it was working.

Clark left for the rink, and I started walking home, digesting the conversation.

To be honest, I wasn't at all sure Al's advice would work with the worst high school hockey team in America. But I *was* convinced it was the only chance I had.

Despite all the warnings, I was committed to doing exactly what I told the search committee I would do: become the state's hardest-working team. I was determined to raise the bar, not lower it.

Whether it would work remained to be seen.

■ If you're a leader, a lot of headaches will come your way, and it's your job to handle them. But leading your people will give your life more meaning, more depth, and a stronger sense of purpose — exactly the things your people long for too. Always remember: leading is not a chore but a privilege.

- Don't try to fool your people. They can smell phoniness a mile away, but they also recognize sincerity and authenticity, and they respect it. That starts with the job interview. If they don't like your honest answers, you might as well find out sooner than later.

- To make it special to be on your team, make it *hard.* The Navy SEALS and the Peace Corps have wait lists because those are missions, not jobs. The right people are *attracted* to the difficulty. They know not everyone can make it, and that's what makes it special.

2

Be Patient with Results, Not Behavior

- Be patient with your team's *results,* but impatient with their *behavior.*

- Establish high standards on day one, then stick to them.

- No, this won't be for everyone — but you don't want everyone. Make that a selling point.

The job was mine — for better or worse.

A few days later I went back to Rod Sorge's cinder-block office in the school basement to ask him everything he knew about the players, the parents, and the program. I took notes while Sorge, the ultimate straight-shooter, laid out the situation without varnish.

"First, the bad news," he told me, pulling out a stat sheet from the previous year. "We scored only thirty-three goals last year" — an anemic 1.3 per game. "And our top three scorers all graduated. Plus our goalie, Brandon Tucker. He was great."

How great? Against state champion Detroit Catholic Central,

Tucker faced seventy-seven shots and stopped seventy — something he did several times that season. In hockey, thirty-five shots is an unusually busy night for a goalie, so these were astronomical numbers. To save 90 percent in such a lopsided game was an extraordinary feat.

"Okay," I said, trying to stay cool. "We graduated our four best players on a team that didn't win a game. That's the bad news. So what's the good news?"

"Who said there was good news?" Sorge replied. "I've got bad news, and I've got *worse* news."

I shook my head. "All right," I said. "Give me the worse news."

Sorge went down the roster, giving me a thumbnail sketch of each player who might be returning. After a while they all started to sound the same: not very big, not very fast, not much talent. The few Sorge identified who had any skill often came with hang-ups of one sort or another — unfocused, undisciplined, uncooperative.

Bobby Chappuis had been a freshman on the previous team. Looking back, he recalls, "We just didn't have the size, speed, skill, or any of the other ingredients needed to win. But what I remember most about that season was the mood. We were deflated, cynical, and didn't seem to think that we *could* win. I've forgotten many of the specifics, but what stuck with me was that the culture was uninspired. We would step on the ice with no confidence, and no mission."

Sorge thought some of them worked hard on the ice but others didn't. Some worked hard in the classroom, some didn't. But he seemed to like them, which, in a sea of minuses, I regarded as a pretty big plus.

"So there you go," Sorge said. "That's what you have to work with. Good luck."

When he snapped his folder shut, he couldn't resist giving me an "I told you so" grin.

• • •

I set up a lunch meeting with Mike Henry, the incoming captain. After I pulled into the parking lot, I saw Henry drive up in his dad's Explorer and get out wearing baggy cargo pants, a T-shirt, and a baseball hat, an All-American high school kid. He held a small piece of paper filled with a short list of items he wanted to discuss.

He didn't seem too happy to see me — but then, like a lot of people, he probably wasn't too happy I had been named the head coach either. Remember, he had been on the search committee, and he'd voted against me. In fairness, Henry knew his job was to advocate for his teammates, and he took his role seriously.

After we sat down, I thanked him for coming and told him I knew he would be absolutely vital to turning this program around. Then, in frank terms, I explained what I needed from him.

"I will judge you solely by your work as captain," I said. "If you don't score a single goal but you lead this team, I'll be happy. If you're the league's top scorer but not the team's leader, we won't go very far." Then I added, with a grin, "A year from now we'll be laughing about this conversation."

Henry didn't crack a smile.

But what I perceived as coldness, Henry recently told me, was mostly anxiety. He had just turned seventeen and had never been to a business meeting or a job interview until the athletic director put him on the search committee. We were asking a lot of him.

I pulled out the plans I had brought in my leather notebook, including a baseline physical test I intended to conduct on Monday, June 26 — the week after school would let out for the summer — to measure where everyone stood on strength, aerobic fitness, running speed, and the like, plus a schedule of summer practices, and more. Henry stared at me, unmoved, taking no notes, and asking no questions.

When I finished my spiel, Henry said, "My turn."

He had not come to listen but to stand up for his downtrodden teammates, a gesture I should have recognized as a sign of authentic leadership. He was literally taking one for the team, risking his status with the new coach to speak up for those who couldn't. But I heard his message as just more defeatism.

Henry pulled out his small sheet with a few points scribbled on it.

The first: "You have no idea what you're getting into," he said, unaware he was quoting Sorge verbatim. Perhaps I should have listened.

Instead, I chuckled. Henry didn't.

His second point underscored his first: the team didn't have much talent. Their best players had graduated, only a few returning players had ever played on a travel team, and some weren't good enough to play for the previous Huron team that couldn't win a game.

"So others have said," I acknowledged.

Henry's third point: "We want it to be fun."

This threw me for a loop, but I kept my composure before replying, "It should be fun, but it should also be more than that."

I wisely held back expressing my next thought: if our only goal is to have fun, perhaps we should just give the players our budget for ice time, buses, coaches, and pucks, and send all of them to Disneyworld — or, more likely, Daytona Beach. But some things were lost in translation — including our definitions of "fun" — which can happen when two strangers approach an entrenched problem from decidedly different angles.

"Don't forget where we were coming from," Henry told me recently. "We didn't *just* want to have fun. But we'd had such a miserable time the year before that if the players didn't try to make the locker room a little fun, then no one would have wanted to come to the rink. It was so dark — *so* dark — that we had to lighten things up."

I had also failed to see things from Henry's point of view — and by proxy, from his teammates' perspective. I had just taken over the team, I hadn't yet lost a single game, and my head was swimming with ideas and optimism. Henry and his teammates, on the other hand, had just survived two years in a program that had produced a lot more dismal days than wins (just three in fifty-two games). They

had been beaten down day by day and week by week by their opponents, their classmates, and sometimes themselves.

If I had gone through all that, I might have been hesitant to believe the best way to end my suffering was to outwork every other
team in the state for four months, before even playing our first
game. And for what? The slim chance of actually winning a hockey
game that winter? These players had fallen for false hope too many
times to dare to believe again. If I had played on that team, I probably wouldn't have been in the mood to hear any sales pitches either, especially from an inexperienced coach they hadn't wanted in
the first place. To them, my hiring was just another example of their
voices not being heard.

I had a lot to learn.

Henry moved to his fourth point: "Lapper's our man," he said,
referring to nineteen-year-old Mike Lapprich, who had played for
Huron before serving as an assistant coach the previous two seasons, while attending community college. "He's our guy. You're
keeping him. Treat him right."

None of these were suggestions.

I had met Lapper six years earlier when he was a freshman on
Huron's team and I was in my last year as an assistant coach. Lapper was a big, strong, hardworking kid with a sweet smile, who ex-
uded a quiet warmth and a strong sense of humor, but only after
you got to know him.

I liked Lapper — who didn't? — but I didn't know how much he
knew about hockey or coaching, or what role he would play on our
staff. I assumed older hockey friends of mine would help run the
team, and perhaps Lapper could take on some lighter duties.

Before I had lunch with Henry I had no idea how much Lapper
meant to the players. But I already knew I could use all the help I
could get, and I've always taken a dim view of managers who clean
house as soon as they get the job. So it wasn't hard for me to assure
Henry, "I have no intention of getting rid of Lapper."

Henry seemed satisfied with that — perhaps the first thing I'd
said that he liked. Before we finished, he agreed to host his team-

mates for a meet-and-greet on his parents' back deck the following week. In the parking lot I thanked him again and shook his hand. He shook mine in silence and climbed back into his Explorer.

I left our meeting with only one firm thought: *I do not have the captain on my side.*

How would I handle his teammates? We'd find out in a few days.

If you're taking over a division, a department, or even an entire organization, you will surely be responsible for the bottom line, however it's measured: profits, production, enrollments, or customer-satisfaction-index (CSI). If the goals are ambitious — and they should be — it will take some time to get there, and doubly so if you're working on a turnaround project. To turn around *performance*, you're going to have to be patient. That's okay. You can afford to be patient if you're going in the right direction.

But going in the right direction means everyone's *behavior* has to support those performance goals. So when it comes to changing *conduct*, you have to be impatient — extremely impatient. You need to spell out your standards of conduct immediately, explain why they're important, and enforce them on day one. Those not willing or able to meet those standards, no matter how great their numbers are, need to know it — and if they simply don't want to, you need to let them go. After all, what you're doing is special, and therefore it won't be for everyone. If you let them keep showing up without meeting your team's standards, you've just told everyone that you really weren't serious about your standards after all, and your word is no good. And now you're cooked.

But if you get this vital first step right, your people will come to understand that the team rules are important and worth following, and they'll actually become *proud* of what those rules represent. When that happens, *they* will begin to enforce the standards, and once they've bought into your culture of hard work and teamwork, it will become self-perpetuating — just like Al Clark told me.

Once your people have embraced your team's standards, you can move on to strategy, tactics, and all the things you'll need to get right to reach your goals. If your values are clear, if your people share them, and if everyone follows them — *including you* — the rest will come relatively easily, and your bottom line will rise faster than anyone would have expected. You and your team can enjoy that success with a clear conscience.

But first, you have to have the guts to tell them how your team is going to work. Because if you don't believe it, don't expect them to.

Here's what *doesn't* work: trying to set standards gradually, cautiously, and fearfully, with a litany of little rules that will drive everyone crazy. When you take over your team, especially if it's a losing one, don't try to ease them into your expectations, in the misplaced belief that somehow you'll persuade them to raise the bar bit by bit.

They will laugh at you. Begging them to dip their toes into the shallow end won't get anyone into the deep end, where the real work gets done.

No, everyone has to dive right into the deep end on day one. This approach might sound tough, but it's actually based on a foundation of respect. It recognizes that your people aren't stupid, they're not lazy, they can handle high standards of conduct, and they can achieve them quickly — faster than their critics think they can.

Most people prefer this approach, and I can prove it with a simple question: Whenever someone tells you, "I've got good news and bad news," which do you ask for first? The bad news, right? That's what your people want too, and they'll respect you for giving it to them straight. They've probably already met the self-proclaimed "laid-back boss" who brags about how cool their culture is, but then tells them they have to work on weekends.

After you lay out your high expectations, then you tell them *why* these things are so important, why they will benefit *everyone*, and why their work, and therefore their lives, will be improved by joining a team that functions at such a high level. And now you start getting them on board.

I didn't institute high standards for my new team immediately because I was on some power trip and got my kicks out of punishing people. Quite the opposite: I wanted to get basic housekeeping issues like showing up on time and dressing appropriately for each workout, practice, and game out of the way so we could work on bigger things like installing sophisticated drills and game strategies.

I wasn't into punishment. I was into *accountability*. Those might sound similar, but they're very different. Punishment is adversarial, based on power, and demeaning for everyone involved. Accountability is collaborative, and it's based on respect. When I tell you to make sure you're ready for the bus before 5:00, I am giving you good advice. The bus didn't leave right on time to punish anyone any more than airplanes leave on time to stick it to late passengers. The bus pulls out right on time *because that's when the bus leaves*. Our approach was actually an invitation to these young men to lead themselves. When you set clear boundaries, you invite people to be their own boss. They can be adults, figure it out, and get there on time.

As I told them, "We always have the option of growing up."

I also told them that if they screwed up, they had only three possible answers: "Yes, sir," "No, sir," or "No excuse, sir." I wasn't interested in hearing anything else. But this approach came with a silver lining: once you gave me one of those answers, we were done with the matter. I wasn't going to rub your nose in it or hold a grudge. The consequences were yours to face, and once you faced them, it was over. We moved on.

Your candor will surprise them. They're not used to that, especially these days, when everyone else is offering them kombucha machines. You're offering them honesty, respect, and a higher sense of purpose. Give them those things, and you'll stand out from the crowd, attract the right people, and earn their undivided attention.

. . .

As soon as I officially got the job, I spent a full day composing, copy-ing, and sending out packets of information in manila envelopes to all the players who had been on the team the previous year, minus the graduating seniors. I inserted a full-page introductory letter, the upcoming season's schedule, and a two-sided questionnaire. On it, I asked them to tell me about their hockey history, what they liked, what they didn't, and what they hoped to experience in the upcom-ing season individually, and as a team. I asked them to return the questionnaire to me when we met at Mike Henry's back deck the following week. If they were going to be out of town, they could drop it in the mail.

There were some unspoken messages in that questionnaire too: Your experience matters. Your opinions matter. Your hopes and dreams matter. *You* matter. And we're all going to need to work to-gether to turn this program around.

In contrast to those unspoken messages, my main points in my opening letter were about as subtle as a sledgehammer between the eyes. That was for a number of reasons, but one of the big ones was this: when the results are as bad as they had been the previous sea-son, it's easy for everyone to blame everyone else and absolve them-selves of any responsibility for the train wreck they just walked away from. While I didn't want anyone to feel guilty, I did want them to realize that when you finish 0-22-3, it's pretty hard for anyone in-volved to claim they were doing a great job.

So in my letter I wanted to be clear as a bell. I wrote,

CONGRATULATIONS!
You have joined the state's hardest working high school hockey team! This is a FIRST-CLASS program.
To be on it, you must conduct yourself in a FIRST-CLASS manner at all times.
THERE WILL BE NO FUZZINESS IN OUR EXPECTATIONS.
THERE WILL BE NO SLOPPINESS IN YOUR CONDUCT.

But the thrust was largely positive. After providing a brief bio, I explained,

We will be guided by two rules: Work hard. Support your teammates.

That's it. Everything else flows from those. If we do those things, I'll be happy — win or lose. And if we don't, I won't be — win or lose.

YOU CAN DEPEND ON YOUR TEAMMATES BECAUSE YOUR TEAMMATES CAN DEPEND ON YOU.

YOU ARE THE MOST IMPORTANT TEAM IN THE HISTORY OF HURON HOCKEY.

I invited them to contact me anytime they wanted, by mail, email, phone, or in person, then closed by saying, "I believe to the bottom of my heart *we can and will* produce a dramatic turnaround in the Huron hockey program."

I wanted them to take away this message: I'll work with you, you work with me, and together we'll go further than we could have imagined.

A week passed without any reaction from anyone. I wasn't sure if I'd already ticked everyone off, if I'd lost them, if they didn't believe me, or if they just didn't care — but I cannot deny that the dead silence got to me. I was walking into an underground cave with a pack of damp matches.

If I flopped before I even got to the starting line, I could console myself that at least I had failed while daring greatly. So I had that going for me.

On Saturday, June 24, I showed up early for the introductory meeting with the players on Mike Henry's back deck, along with my friend Ned Glysson (pronounced "Gliss-en"), who had been doing a great job leading our adult league team for years. I was hoping he would join our staff.

I started chatting with the few players who got there early, but most straggled in late, unapologetic, and looking sloppy. Only *two* of the dozen or so guys who showed up handed me their filled-out questionnaires, as I'd requested in my introductory letter.

"Almost nobody did it, including me," Henry recalls. "When the fourth guy didn't have it and I saw you were getting pissed, I quietly snuck upstairs, filled it out in a hurry, and handed it in."

Well, that made three. What would I do about that? I had no plan.

At exactly one o'clock, I introduced myself — even as guys were still walking up — told them a bit of my background, and then requested they do the same. As we went around the U-shaped bench, I asked each player a question or two, and I remembered their names. When the last player finished, I went back around the bench, recited all of their names, plus a few things about each guy, to show them that I'd been listening and that they mattered to me.

Then I shifted gears, letting my instincts take over.

"Three of you returned your questionnaires. Thank you for that. This will help me get to know you better, and to coach you better.

"As for the rest of you, why didn't you? Was there any fuzziness in my expectations? Anything not clear? Was it too hard? Not enough time? Did any of you call or email with questions? I included all my contact information."

Their eyes widened, and they straightened their backs.

Our best returning player, junior-to-be Jon "Elmo" Eldredge, later told me, "We did what we thought was expected of us — and that was to fail, and fail epically. You were pissed, and rightfully so."

I wasn't finished, now rolling with a head of steam. "Gentlemen, *this* is the problem. *This* is why you haven't won a game in a year and a half. We want to bring in systems from the nation's best programs — but if we can't finish something this easy, we don't stand a chance of accomplishing *anything*. If you want different results, you'll have to do things differently — starting with completing simple tasks. *And this is a simple task.*

"I wrote those questions so I can get to know you better, as hockey players, and as people, so I can coach you better. Like I wrote in my letter, I'm convinced we can turn this around—but *you* will be the ones who do it, and *you* will be the ones who get the credit for doing it too.

"Aren't you sick of losing? Aren't you sick of getting pounded? Aren't you sick of being the laughingstock of the state, the league, the school? How do you think we're going to change all that if we can't do *this?*" I said, waving the three completed questionnaires in my hand.

"I think you're better than that—and I think we can prove our doubters wrong too. Think how *great* it will feel to win your first game. Your second game. Your *third* game. What it will feel like to *beat Pioneer High School?!* Imagine walking down the hallways of Huron High in your hockey jacket and getting high-fives instead of insults?

"We can do all that. But it's up to you.

"Now, I *know* we can do better than this—and *we have to.* You are capable of much more—but you need to prove it. When we meet in the weight room in two days, on Monday, June 26, at noon, I expect you to hand me your questionnaires. *All of you.*

"Any questions?"

I waited. No hands went up.

"No? Okay. Then we have an understanding. No excuses."

They were now fully alert.

"See you Monday, June 26, at the weight room. *Noon means noon.*"

Yes, I was hanging it out there pretty far, especially in our first ten minutes together. But it's important to note what I *didn't* do: yell, scream, or shame them. I laid out the facts—about where we were, what getting better would require, and what it would look like —and the *facts* made the case for me. That's all you need.

"You're free to go," I said to the silent bunch. "But seniors, stick around if you can. I want your help designing our new home uniforms."

That last line created a little buzz. Their old uniforms were a dog's breakfast of two logos, a rat in hockey gear laid over a stylized "H," made of bad material, with the wrong Huron "H" and the wrong colors too. Huron's colors are forest green and old gold—just like the NHL's Dallas Stars in their heyday—but the old uniforms were a bland green and light yellow. I hated everything about those jerseys. Luckily, they were old enough to replace. Although the program had only $2,000 in the bank, I had faith we'd raise the money before the bill came due.

There was a message in designing new uniforms too: we were going to have a new look, a new status for seniors, and a new collaboration between us. In short, I was expecting *them* to start leading, from day one.

We spent twenty minutes drawing up our new uniforms. Then Coach Ned and I walked down Henry's driveway toward my car, by ourselves. Once we were out of earshot, I whispered to Ned, "Well, that got their attention." We chuckled nervously, shaking our heads. I added, "By next week, *you* might be the head coach."

Henry recalls, "You turned a meet-and-greet into the first slap in the face. It was awkward and put us on our heels. Simple message: get on board—or get out."

I might have overshot the mark. I didn't want to make it awkward, or slap them in the face if I could avoid it. But I also didn't want to try to lead a bunch of individuals who couldn't complete an easy assignment that was intended to help *them*.

Walking away from our first team meeting, everyone knew this much: the gauntlet had been dropped. Things were going to change, for better or for worse.

But we were not going to be the same.

■ **If you plan to change the culture where you work, you need to separate *behavior* from *results*. Turning around results takes time, and you'll need to be patient. But changing group behavior needs to be done *immediately*, so you have to be *impatient*. If your people can't handle** basic expectations, they won't be able to handle the complicated tasks they'll need to master later. There will be times when you make rare exceptions down the road, but not at first. Start with the small things and get them right.

- Don't expect to coax your people from the shallow end to the deep end. They won't go. Better to have everyone jump into the deep end right from the start.

- Tell them the "bad news" first, including your high expectations and all the hard work and sacrifice your mission is going to require, then explain why this will not be for everyone. If they're still listening, you can tell them the good news: this new approach will work, the rewards will be exceptional, and the journey will be deeply satisfying.

- You won't get everyone on board with this approach, but you don't want everyone. This is a great way to weed out the posers from the real workers—and you'll be pleasantly surprised just how many people come with you, eyes wide open.

3

─────

Learning How to Count

- If you live in fear of being fired, you'll never be a great leader.

- The harder we work, the harder it is to surrender, the bigger we can dream.

- Don't apologize for high expectations. *Celebrate* them.

Monday, June 26 — one week after school let out for the summer.

I arrived with Coach Lapper, the nineteen-year-old assistant, at the Huron weight room thirty minutes before our noon workout to set up twelve stations, a combination of machines and some free weights. I would have the players pair up, with one of them working the weight machine and the other stretching while counting out their partner's reps, up to ten. After they alternated two sets each, they'd move on to the next station, with no lag time in between, and everybody would keep moving.

I'm no fan of folks sitting on weight benches, staring at themselves in the mirror — an all too common scene at your local gym. If we're going to work out, let's work out, not stand around admiring ourselves. If we worked efficiently, I estimated, we'd finish the entire weight workout in about thirty minutes, then head outside to the track for thirty more minutes of sprints and other hockey-specific exercises.

I also put a stack of forms on the table so the players could write in their maxes for squats, bench presses, curls, and the like, to establish their physical baselines. At the end of the workout I would give them individualized programs to do on their own that summer, then I'd see them again when school started. We'd see how they'd progressed, and we'd know where we stood in terms of conditioning. That was my plan, anyway.

I also brought pens, because I already knew they would not be bringing those. I was prepared for that. But I was not prepared for what happened next.

About fifteen guys showed up, representing most of the returning players, and on time. Most of them brought their questionnaires, filled out. Progress.

I made a show of watching the clock and starting exactly at noon. When the sweep hand hit 12:00, I bellowed, "Welcome to Huron hockey's workout! Thanks for coming."

For merely turning in the questionnaires, I gave them fulsome praise.

"See? You can do this — and a lot more. Nice work!"

They seemed to take some quiet pride in this small accomplishment, but they were not about to take the bait of hope and allow themselves to believe they were going to accomplish anything on the ice that year. We were miles from that.

I also praised them for showing up on time, then dropped a few bombs:

"We are going to be the hardest-working high school hockey team in the state. You will be the most important team in school history — the one that saves the program and turns it around. Our goal is nothing less than *winning the state title*."

I paused to take in their mix of alarm and amusement. *Is this guy crazy?*

"It won't be this year," I added, "but that's what we're shooting for, starting *today*. When we get there, not too long from now, the team that does it will have our first team — *you guys* — to thank. And they'll give you a standing ovation at that banquet."

They thought I was nuts, but my vision got their attention.

Then I asked the seniors-to-be, led by Mike Henry, to form a small inner circle, and everyone else to form a bigger circle around them. Just setting this up took two minutes. Then I showed them the stretches I wanted them to do, nothing fancy, and told them I wanted the seniors to shout out the odd numbers, and everyone else to shout out the even numbers, like this:

Seniors: "One!"
Others: "Two!"
Seniors: "Three!"
Others: "Four!"

And so on, up to ten for each stretch. Simple stuff, right?

I expected them to be loud, quick, sharp, and intense — but they were the opposite in every respect. The seniors felt embarrassed to demonstrate the slightest bit of enthusiasm. They would mumble the number, say it a beat behind, or not say anything, while making faces at each other and giggling awkwardly at the silliness of it all. They were too cool to care, and this exercise, as far as they were concerned, was for dorks.

"That was exactly it," Henry told me years later, when I started writing this book. "We really did want to win, and we expected to work. We just didn't know how to get there. It was *definitely* not cool to care — a very accurate statement."

These guys weren't about to fall for any rah-rah stuff. I suspected that keeping an ironic distance was their coping mechanism to mitigate the pain of failure. Going 0-22-3 when no one cared? That was kind of cool in a way, something you could joke about at school dances. But what if you really worked and sacrificed for months, and even showed everyone you cared, and *then* you lost every game? Not so cool. That would leave a bruise.

One of our two senior goalies, Steve Beltran, said it best years later: "We thought it was hilarious that we didn't win a game. We had no pride — or our pride had been so broken down over the course of that season that we didn't want to admit that our pride was hurt. Looking back, it was embarrassing."

Whatever the cause, I was still stunned by how pathetic the effort was. *They weren't even trying.* When I gave Lapper a look of exasperation, he just shrugged. He'd been through the 0-22-3 season with these guys and was far harder to shock than I was.

After a few minutes, I couldn't take it anymore. I stopped them. I told them briefly what I had just seen, and then at length what I expected to see. I demonstrated how to stretch, while barking every number — alternating the odds and evens by turning my head left and right — and then told them to try it again.

They simply couldn't do it. Or wouldn't do it — and I wasn't sure which was worse. But despite my frustration, I refused to take over the world's simplest drill, just to make sure we did it right. After all, *I* knew how to do it — but I wouldn't be playing that year. They were the ones who had to learn it — and had to *teach others* to do it.

So I made them try it again.

And again.

And again.

By the time we finally stretched and counted with enough enthusiasm and competence to satisfy me, it was already 12:20 — and I'm confident they were now as sick of me as I was of them.

We didn't have enough time to do the rest of our exercises, but the few they did were a failure too. After our opening stretches, they paired up to lift weights. I told the partners who weren't lifting to stretch while spotting and counting to ten for their partners who were working the machines, then switch. But they could not do this elementary drill correctly either.

"Do it again," was the mantra of the day.

Just forty-five minutes into our first workout I knew that my original plan — giving them a baseline test and a workout program, then sending them off to work out on their own for the rest of the summer — was foolhardy. If they couldn't even stretch and count properly while closely supervised by two coaches, I didn't have to wonder what they would do without any coaches at all.

I realized I would have to recalibrate my sights, and quickly, before they left for the day. Once they had gone home, I wasn't sure if I could ever get them back.

If my original plan wouldn't work, I decided the principles behind it still would. But if I was going to ask more of them, I would have to ask more of myself. To make any progress that off-season, which I believed was essential to turning things around that winter, I concluded I would have to supervise every workout, three days a week, in the weight room and out on the track, from noon until 1:30, all summer long.

At the end of that first day, I called them together, told them the new plan, and closed with, "See you on Wednesday. And don't forget: *noon means noon!*"

When I got home, I canceled my summer plans and emailed everyone our new schedule of summer workouts, three times a week.

At our next workout two days later, I asked captain Mike Henry to lead the stretching. No luck. It was all jokes, a wink and a nod to his teammates to let them know that he thought it was just as stupid as they did. Once again, however, instead of taking it over I asked Henry to do it again, and again, and again, until we achieved something close to what I was looking for.

After spending too much time on stretching once more, I let them pick their partners for lifting. Henry picked his best friend, Steve Beltran, and things went downhill from there. After that, I learned to pick their partners for them, matching upperclassmen with underclassmen, to break down barriers and to head off the potential problems some pairings presented.

But none of this improved my relationships with captain Mike Henry; our top player, Jon "Elmo" Eldredge; or our goalie, Steve Beltran.

After one of our workouts, I said to Lapper, half-joking, "My captain voted for the other guy, my best player's head is somewhere else, and my starting goalie hates being here. How am I doing?"

At each workout our top returning player, Elmo, a funny, popular guy with wavy, perfectly unkempt rock-star hair, would occasionally peel off from his lifting partner to stand by himself on the side, staring off into space. I had the sense that he wasn't being flaky, that still waters ran deep with him. Teenage angst was the most likely culprit.

I was sympathetic but didn't think less structure and accountability would help someone already feeling adrift. I knew that I wanted more out of him, that he could deliver, and that it would do him good.

One day when Elmo didn't show up for our workout, I asked Mike Henry if he knew where he was.

"My house," Henry said. "He slept over."

"So," I said, confused, "why isn't he here now?"

"He was still sleeping when I left."

I blinked. "You didn't think to wake him up?"

"I tried," he said, shrugging. It wasn't his problem. Before Henry had left early that morning to run an errand, Elmo told him he had a backup ride, then went back to sleep.

These workouts were voluntary, but I had reached my limit. "Call him," I said.

Henry didn't like having to make the call, but Elmo liked being called even less.

When Henry hung up, he said, "Elmo's ride fell through. He sounded pretty annoyed."

"With *you?*" I said, incredulous.

"No, with *you*," Henry said.

It was my turn to shrug. If Elmo was irritated by being woken up before the crack of noon, I could get over that.

"Tell Elmo to get here as fast as he can," I said, knowing the Henrys lived close to the school.

When Elmo eventually showed up, halfway through our workout, he was genuinely surprised to find I wasn't very understanding.

As Elmo recently recalled, "I had to walk to practice that day. Not too terribly far, but I was certainly late getting there. I figured the circumstances of my tardiness would earn me a pass. Shocker: it didn't."

At that moment I was pretty pissed off, but unsure what to do about it. Part of me thought maybe I should forget about turning the program around. Forget about winning a game. We couldn't even manage to show up on time and count to ten — something kindergartners manage to do every day. I was only thirty-five, but I felt like an old man barking at kids to get off my lawn.

I decided yelling at Elmo might only chase him off, and then he could be gone forever. I calmed down and helped the other guys for the rest of the workout. But when I sensed they were watching me, wondering what I was going to do about Elmo, I decided I had to make a public statement to reinforce the importance of the character and culture we were trying to instill during these workouts.

When we finished, I thanked them for coming, underscored all that we'd accomplished that day, and said I'd see them back in the weight room in two days. I was sticking with the facts, as I would with Elmo: "And don't forget, Elmo: *noon means noon.*"

He gave me a look, which I expected. I hadn't gone on a tirade, but even that little mention could have been enough for him to decide, *Screw this. I'm outta here.*

I honestly had no idea if I would see Elmo again. I had no idea if his friends were going to follow me or follow him. He was a very popular guy, after all, and they knew him a lot better than they knew me. I'm sure they liked him better too. Honestly, I wasn't sure if I'd get fired at the end of our first season, during it, or even before we played our first game that winter.

But I was certain of this: if we couldn't get going in time for a noon workout, it wouldn't matter who was coaching. Huron hockey would be going nowhere – again.

I'm not trying to be flip. But in the early stages of a cultural revolution, it's almost entirely on you, the coach, the CEO, the division manager, to set the compass, make the tough decisions, and then stand by them. To do that you have to be able to answer a single, simple question: are you willing to risk getting fired? Because once your people know you're holding back to save your job, they will too.

If you're more afraid of losing your job than doing a poor job, you'll definitely do a poor job, and you might lose your job anyway. Then what do you have?

To lead effectively, you have to be willing to be fired. You have to be willing to lose one of your stars, or a game, or a fiscal quarter. If you don't stand for your principles, your people will know you don't stand for anything. And who wants to follow a leader like that?

A few weeks into my tenure our incoming captain, Mike Henry, still had more pull with most of the players than I did, though I don't think he recognized it. That wouldn't have been a problem if we were pulling in the same direction. But he was trying to protect his teammates from enduring another miserable year, while I was trying to turn the program around. Initially we did not always see those goals as being compatible.

A few times we stepped on each other's toes. It's one thing for a seventeen-year-old kid to do that, especially when he's standing up for his buddies. But it's quite another for a thirty-five-year-old head coach to do it, occasionally in front of the team. Those are two big no-no's in any era, but being behind the norms of the time compounded some of my mistakes. For example, too often I resorted to a sledgehammer when a fly swatter would have sufficed. These were all rookie mistakes I learned to correct, but they cost me in the short run.

For all these reasons, the captain and I were not on the same page. When I asked Henry to lead stretches, he invariably chuckled and rolled his eyes. I assumed he didn't like our workouts and wasn't doing much to hide it — and the younger guys picked up on it. In Henry's defense, I hadn't designed the workouts for fun. They were created with a higher purpose in mind.

"We weren't just practicing like you play," recalls former player Scooter McConnell. "We were practicing *harder* than you play. We weren't used to being pushed that hard, and not everyone was on board at first. When someone asked why we were doing all these things we hadn't done the year before, Bacon didn't miss a beat. 'Because you guys sucked last year.' Everyone laughed, and it broke the tension. Then he got more serious and said, 'If you want different results, you have to do things differently.' When we ran around the track, Bacon would yell, 'No one will work harder than we will!' He wasn't joking. I don't think anyone could have."

Henry attended every workout, but his lack of seriousness, which I interpreted as both disregard for our work and disrespect for me, was getting old. Finally, four weeks after our first workout, I asked him to arrive thirty minutes beforehand so we could talk. I was prepared to serve my customary "praise sandwich," consisting of praise-criticism-praise, or more accurately: praise, a call to action, and more praise.

Henry arrived on time — and yes, it mattered. I told him he was a smart, popular guy, but more importantly for our purposes, he had natural charisma — he was a born leader.

"But the problem is," I explained, "you don't realize it. If you go this way, twenty kids go with you. If you go that way, twenty kids go that way. But you don't see them following you. So if you're screwing around, or rolling your eyes, or laughing, they assume that whatever we're doing must not be important. Whenever I bring this to your attention, you've always got an answer. Whether you like it or not, Captain, you're a leader. *But you have to start acting like it.*"

I asked him if he got the point, and he nodded.

"I inherited a captain," I said, "but I don't have to. I need you. This team needs you. But if you're not going to go the right direction, we can pick another captain who will. *I need you to lead.*"

Years later Henry told me, "I didn't see this meeting as a confrontation, but more of a first step toward understanding each other. I didn't realize the power I had. You showed me the ability I had to lead in a positive way. That was a big lesson for me."

Of course, I didn't know if any of that had sunk in at the time, so I had no idea how Henry would respond. But I did know I felt a hell of a lot better. I'd laid out the facts, and all of it was true, so the rest was up to him.

Here's the thing: if I wasn't as candid with my captain as I could be, I'd be doing him a grave disservice. If we were going to lead this team together, he needed all the information I had, unfiltered, to help him do so. To do otherwise would leave him in the dark and, really, insult him, because the message then is, "You can't handle it." Mike Henry struck me as strong, and I believed he could handle it — but we would see.

I've seen this many times in the corporate world: people aren't leading because they don't realize they are *expected* to lead, and that they *can* lead. Show them they can lead, tell them your team needs them to, and you're halfway home.

In Henry's case, we were about to find out if he *wanted* to. He could have given up or gone home. Instead, a few minutes after our talk he led his teammates in the opening stretching exercise better than he ever had. He kept it up too, growing bigger in the role week by week.

I'm convinced the key was that meeting. If I had complained to *anyone else* about Henry's flippant attitude, it would have gotten back to him, and then our relationship would have been forever damaged. Our team could have gone under before we even got started. I was convinced Henry's leadership was that important to our future.

Challenging your top leader to get moving or to move aside is not guaranteed to magically solve your leadership problem. But I'm just as confident it's your best chance — and sometimes your only chance.

About the same time Henry and I had our summit meeting, I was also getting fed up with his best friend, Steve Beltran, one of two re-turning senior goalies. If Elmo looked like the lead singer of a rock band, Beltran could have played lead guitar — a lean kid with long-ish brown hair and lots of edgy energy. He was funny, engaging, and confident, with the kind of swagger you want in a goalie, the tough-est position in any sport.

Beltran wasn't mean-spirited, and his soccer teammates were sufficiently impressed to make him their team captain. But his con-fidence sometimes translated as cockiness, his humor as sarcasm, and he had the knack of pushing things right up to the line during our workouts. After a few weeks of his wisecracks and half-assed effort, I had grown tired of monitoring him just to make sure he didn't cross the line. I was developing an itchy trigger finger, so it wasn't going to take much to set me off.

Early in our workout on Friday, August 4, while I was encour-aging a friend of Beltran's in the squat rack, Beltran laughed at the lack of weights on the bar, and that's all it took. Without any prepa-ration or premeditation, I pulled Beltran aside, looked him straight in the eye, and said, "Steve, I don't think you want to be here, and you're not getting much out of it. That's your problem. But you're distracting others, and that's *my* problem. So I think you need to go home."

All the cool drained from his face that instant.

"*What?*"

"I said: You need to go home. You're off the team."

He stammered a bit, but eventually made his way out the door, stunned.

Looking back on it, Beltran told me, "I remember being shocked and angry after getting kicked out. 'How dare this guy kick me off the team! Who does he think he is?' At first, all I could do was blame you for my actions."

When the remaining players finished lifting, I gathered everyone before we ran outside to the track. I felt they needed to know that my decision, although spontaneous, wasn't rash or random, and that if they were working hard and supporting their teammates, they had nothing to worry about.

"Steve wasn't meeting our standards," I said. "So I sent him home."

I was surprised when a few of them nodded, perhaps borne of their own quiet frustration. They liked Beltran, but no one wants to work under a double standard. There's a lesson in that too: people who are playing by the rules might not call out a peer who isn't, but they're often relieved when the leader does.

Two days later, on Sunday night, I got a call from Steve's mom. We had a polite conversation, but I suggested she ask Steve why I had sent him home. If he wanted to get back on the team, I said, he could call me himself. The rest was up to him — and again, there was no way of knowing what he'd do.

Steve called a few minutes later, sounding contrite — not a posture that came readily to him at that age. We talked briefly about what had happened, what needed to change, and if he was willing to deliver. He said all the right things, and I strongly sensed he meant them. Satisfied, I invited him back on the team for the next day's workout, telling him again that I believed he could be a great contributor, and that we needed him — all true. He sounded quite relieved, and the next day his attitude was much improved.

When I was writing this book, Beltran sent me a few pages of great stories, memories, and insights. "You came in hot those first few months," he wrote, in what was probably a diplomatic under-statement, "and a lot of us weren't happy about it."

Beltran and others said one key was Lapper, who often served as the middleman between me and the players. Lapper not only kept Henry, Elmo, and Beltran in the tent when they might have bolted, he provided a quiet assurance to everyone that this new regime was worth joining, that they mattered, and that he would always have their backs.

"Any anger or resentment we felt towards you could be voiced to him," Beltran says today. "I think a lot of that had to do with Lap-prich being there to talk me off the ledge that summer. He was al-ways the voice of reason. He essentially confirmed that I was be-ing an ass and needed to grow up. For whatever reason, it sounded different coming from him. We felt like he was one of us, and if he was buying in, maybe we should too. It really helped with the tran-sition.

"Removing me set the tone for future workouts. It also helped me realize I needed to grow up and be a better leader. I don't re-member holding any grudge [toward you] once the season started. In the end, the anger shifted to respect."

If they had Lapper, I had my vision and my principles. My play-ers would probably be surprised to hear it, but I frequently ques-tioned if I'd been too hard here or too soft there, and I often wasn't sure what to do next. But I never questioned that the foundation of our rebuilding project had to be based on character and culture. Knowing that allowed me to be more decisive. If I screwed up here or there, I could make the necessary adjustments, and occasional apologies, just so long as I kept our true north in my sights.

I never had another problem with Beltran, who became one of our strongest leaders. Everyone else got the message too: if I was willing to send one of our top two goalies home, absolutely nobody was bigger than the team.

．　．　．

I need to be clear that in confronting these players I was not playing some sort of Jedi mind-trick, as if I could somehow hypnotize
them by getting into their heads, calling their bluffs, and make them
go my way.

Quite the opposite. My conflicts with all three players represented sizable risks, without any guarantee of how they might respond. By throwing down the gauntlet, I knew I could lose them — a
loss that would be damaging to the team's chances and our overall
chemistry. Their departures could have sparked a mutiny, since so
many players were already considering quitting before I was hired,
and these guys had sway. It would also have bothered me personally. I don't like firing people, and some of their behaviors aside, I
already liked them, even if they didn't like me. But I couldn't let any
of that cause me to compromise our team's values.

No leader can be so blinded by their people's stature that they're
afraid to make tough decisions — and nothing can ever come before
the principles that guide your team.

It helped that most of our players "got it" almost from the start,
and their enthusiasm and confidence grew week by week. I tried
not to let getting the strays back in the pack come at the expense of
the herd, because the herd counts too — and you forget that at your
peril.

New York Yankees manager Casey Stengel once observed: "The
secret of managing is to keep the guys who hate you away from the
guys who are undecided."

I worked hard to keep the guys who were undecided as happy as
I could.

Besides, if some people were not interested in meeting the same
standards that everyone else was *exceeding* on a daily basis, keeping those strays inside the tent would be risky too, especially because they were talented players with magnetic personalities — real
leaders. If I compromised my principles just to keep the strays, the
other guys who were already working their tails off for each other
could be demoralized by the double standard, or drop their own

standards, or both. If that happened, I'd be in danger of losing the entire team.

Given these possibilities, there were no risk-free options. So I figured I might as well stick to my principles and hope everyone rose to the occasion. Whatever happened next *would be up to them.* The leaders draw the lines. Their people decide what they're going to do within them.

Here's the key: If the players walked away, it'd be their choice. If they decided to stay and meet our standards, that would be their choice too. And if they started leading the team, that would *also* be their choice. That's why, if they chose the latter, *they would get all the credit.*

We still had a long way to go. "We were an awful team, a bunch of misfits from District 5," Beltran said, referencing the classic hockey movie *The Mighty Ducks.*

Despite it all, I never believed the players I'd inherited were lazy, stupid, or hopeless. I never lost faith that we were all going to "get it" and take off. I truly believed it was just a question of when.

Why did I think that? Because that first summer *they kept coming back to our workouts,* three times a week, something they had never done before. And after a month Henry and the seniors started leading our stretching on their own. Not with great enthusiasm perhaps, but we had finally achieved basic competence.

I wasn't lowering the bar here, handing out trophies just for showing up. State rules mandated that these workouts were voluntary — and we followed those rules. Family vacations, jobs, and other sports were all good excuses for not showing up. Even if they just didn't feel like attending, I couldn't do anything about it. I promised we would not consider their off-season workout attendance during tryouts, and I meant it. Every year we took a few players who had not worked out with us. I did tell them, however, that we'd designed the workouts specifically to improve hockey performance, so the more they attended the better they'd get—and we would see that during tryouts. But it was all up to them.

That's why it impressed me so much that they kept showing up whether it was hot or cold, windy, raining, or, later, snowing, without any guarantee they would win one game in the coming year—or that they'd even make the team. I learned something else about them too: some of them might have thought the counting-and-stretching bit was too corny and "rah-rah," but they never complained about the actual work. They just didn't want to look like they were enjoying it—thus all the attitude I witnessed, which was largely for the benefit of their buddies.

That might not sound like a very high standard either, but if you'd joined us for one of these workouts, you'd know that just getting through one of them meant something. After forty-five minutes of nonstop weight training, we would run out of the school, yelling and screaming, toward the football stadium steps, then run those at full speed. Next were hockey-specific exercises on the outdoor track—such as running on one leg for a hundred yards, then the other—followed by a relay drill for fifteen minutes that required everyone to run their fastest for the team to succeed. We finished back in the gym with wall-sits, which will test anyone.

"I thought I knew what it was like to work hard before that summer," Scooter McConnell recalls. "But I hadn't seen anything like this. It was never unsafe, but you pushed all of us beyond what we thought our limits were."

Then we'd find our new limits and surpass *those*. Our assistant coach Dale Rominski laid out the paradox perfectly when he told them: "We just did our best—and we can do better." Then we would.

"After some of our workouts, I could barely walk upstairs," goalie Nate Reichwage recalls. "During the three years I played for Huron, I puked twice during workouts—the only times I've ever puked working out. I was by no means out of shape either. That is how grueling some of those workouts really were. We may not have been the most talented hockey team in the state, but win or lose, we knew that we had done everything within our power to prepare for the season."

Months later, during our winter season, to motivate them before the third period of a close game I needed only to ask them who had thrown up during one of our summer workouts. Every hand would go up—including Lapper's and mine.

"Great," I would say. "I ruined your summer. Now go ruin their night."

And they would.

So what was happening here in terms of leadership?

First, the players' extraordinary effort produced not only greater strength and stamina but mental toughness, pride, and camaraderie. They were also learning to define themselves instead of letting the world do it for them. Hall of Fame basketball coach John Wooden once said, "Be more concerned with your character than your reputation, because your character is what you really are, while your reputation is merely what others think you are."

I boiled that down to my mom's oft-repeated line, "Your character is what you do when you think no one's watching." I said it so often that years later my second captain hung a sign with this saying over his door, and his brother—who played lacrosse, not hockey—has made it one of his company's core values.

"Well," I would tell our guys after we ran outside to the school track, "no one's watching us now. Trust me. What we do now is who we are—and we'll take that with us all season. *We decide who we are—no one else.*"

For a group of young men who had been disparaged by almost everyone inside and outside the program, that had to come as welcome news. The slate was clean. Except for my one retort—"You guys sucked last year"—we never made fun of their record. We were starting fresh. And the only things that mattered were working hard and supporting our teammates. Instead of feeling like a pack of losers, we felt like we had created a secret society of dedicated athletes on a noble mission.

"Implied in those high expectations was the sense that you believed in us," Scooter McConnell recalls. "After all, there would be no point in setting a standard we couldn't meet. When you haven't won a game in over a year, it feels good to be accomplishing anything, even if it's on a high school track with no one watching. We took it as a point of pride that we kept going. Once you show yourself you can do a little bit more just once, you know you can do it again, and that's what we did.

"It didn't take long before people bought in, and most of us looked forward to the workouts. We were soon pushing each other as much as Coach pushed us, but we were also hanging out and talking after we were done. We were all friends before those workouts started, but they definitely brought us closer together."

"Look, I hated those workouts," Elmo admits today, "but seeing my teammates flying around the track made it easier. I might be miserable, but I'm not alone because I have my teammates and my coaches working next to me."

I never saw our work as "me against them," but rather "us against the world," or against the weights, the clock, or our rivals in absentia — whatever motivated us that day. Everything we asked them to do, from lifting weights to running sprints to our weekly summer ice times, Lapper and I did with them. I honestly never knew how much that mattered to them until I started soliciting their help for this book.

We made it a point to laugh a lot too — often at my expense. When we'd gather at the starting line for our next sprint, I'd give them another story, slogan, or mantra, then send them off on a full-speed sprint, with me at the back of the pack. Initially I was in better shape than they were (that was the problem), so I'd start picking them off, one by one, gently shouldering each guy I passed while barking, "Fat old man coming through!" They laughed, but they got the point: if I can do it, you can too. I wanted to make our workouts as fun as possible and let them know we were in this together.

Lapper and I tried to be "relentlessly positive," a phrase we often used, and we prodded our people to do the same. We were undeniably demanding, but our message was: This is how winning teams work. It's hard, but *we know you can do it.*

Our players were the most beaten-down athletes in America. The last thing they needed was to hear how much they stunk. They already believed it anyway, chanting their winless record at school dances. Our goal was to get them to believe the opposite of all that: that they were *smart*, they were getting *good*, and they were *tough* — and getting tougher every day. They could handle all this demanding work, and far more.

We must have said "Good work!" a hundred times a day, plus a few other messages we hammered home every time we met:

"You're the hardest-working high school team in the state!"

"Our rivals can't do this — but you can!"

"Work hard! Support your teammates!"

"You play for Huron — it's harder over here!"

"Finish strong!"

And if anyone got negative — which happened a lot in the early days — we'd cut that off with: "That's loser talk!" It had some humor to it, and when it caught on, they soon added a wave of the hand, as if to banish the negativity to the winds.

We weren't blowing smoke either. We were compiling more evidence of their progress in the weight room and on the track every week and using it as proof. After each workout, I sent out emails to the players and parents, listing our exercises, our results, and what team workout records we just broke, highlighting their best efforts. In return the players sent me a steady stream of email and instant messages — in the days before text messages — and I'd always try to respond quickly. I was getting to know them, and they were getting to know me — and we were actually starting to trust each other.

. . .

Before long, the guys were pushing each other in the weight room, on the track, and during our last drill, the infamous wall-sits. "Sitting" with your back flat against the wall in an invisible chair, with your hips and knees at ninety degrees, is an essential exercise for skating, which relies primarily on strong quad muscles.

At first none of them could last more than a minute before their legs started wobbling and they collapsed. (Try it. It's hard.) But three times a week they gave it everything they had: sitting against the wall with their eyes closed, sweat dripping down their faces, pulling something extra from deep inside to squeeze out another ten or twenty seconds as I barked out the times. They eventually passed a minute, then two minutes, until one of them, Ben Lutzeier, reached the five-minute mark. Then he put a twenty-five-pound plate on his lap to make it even harder — something I'd never thought of. *Crazy*.

Ben was soon joined by fellow senior Jake Ramsey. "When everyone but Ben had given up and I kept going," Ramsey says, "I remember you screaming, 'You freshmen, look at this! *This* is dedication.' I was shaking uncontrollably and seconds away from puking, but it gave me the confidence to feel like I was leading by example and to know that you recognized effort and leadership on and off the ice. Conditioning drills were about stamina, yes, but they were also about reminding us that we were putting in hard work other teams weren't, and you were trying to give us a competitive edge."

By early August, just about every guy at our workouts could last five minutes, and then they started adding plates like Lutzeier did. We made a big deal out of that too.

Despite all the worrisome reports I'd gotten about them when I took the job, they started exceeding expectations in ways I hadn't even imagined. I had woefully underestimated them.

They didn't always like it when I was pushing them early on, but before long they were pushing each other along too.

"Keep going!"

"You got this!"

"Don't stop now!"

"Finish strong!"

One of my favorite workouts occurred a few weeks after captain Mike Henry and I had our meeting. There had been a torrential rain that morning, followed by 90 degrees of brutal sunshine and suffocating humidity. When we stood at the starting line of the track to begin our timed relays, a thick steam rose from the black rubber track.

"Gentlemen," I said, "look at the goalposts." The air shimmered so much we could barely make them out at the end of the football field.

"That's right," I said. "This is the hottest day of the year, and this is the hottest hour of the hottest day. And we're *lucky* enough to be running our relays at *exactly the right time!* Another team would *whine* about this. They'd *cry* about this. And they'd probably give up. But that's not you. We're not merely going to run through all this, we're going to *break every record we've set on this track!* Remember, the Navy SEALS don't *whine* about the weather. They *brag* about it. And that's who *we* are."

This pumped up most of the guys.

"Yeah!"

"Let's do this!"

But one of the sophomores, who had joined our workouts just the previous week, groaned. When captain Henry heard this, he turned and repeated one of our mantras, with just the right amount of humor, "Hey! You play for Huron, and *it's harder over here.*"

Boom! That was *exactly* what I'd been waiting to hear, and all the better that it came from Henry, who had the team's respect. He was beginning to recognize his leadership ability, to use it effectively, and to understand that the "rah-rah bullshit," as he called it, was necessary to motivate people to do their best. And really, it wasn't rah-rah at all. It was simply being brave enough to care, and to let it show.

We weren't trying to minimize how hard this would be. We weren't apologizing for it either. We were no longer even selling it. We were *celebrating* it!

I used a lot of slogans, so it was interesting to see which ones stuck. Once Henry said, *You play for Huron, and it's harder over here,* everyone started saying it. That winter we would put that phrase on a sign on our locker-room wall, and we referred to it constantly.

And yes, that day on the steamy track we broke every record we had. It wasn't even close — and they were proud to do it.

"The track is where I believe it all started coming together," Henry recalls. "The team was close, our leaders were doing it with us, and the coaches and the team came together."

Henry fails to mention that he was the captain making all that happen.

They were already beginning to lead themselves.

After a month of hard work, the players started bragging to their friends about how intense our workouts were. Before our first summer ended, some of their friends who played other sports asked our guys if they could join our workouts. When our players passed on their request to me, I shrugged.

"I don't know," I said, milking it for all it was worth. "Do you really think they're tough enough to do what you do?" They laughed, and they beamed. My guys had no trouble divining the deep respect embedded in my answer. "Hey, you guys have already put in twenty killer workouts, and your friends are just starting. Remember your first workout? Now look at what you're doing today. So tell you what: I'll leave it up to you. You need to ask *them* if *they* can hack it. We don't need your buddies dying on our track."

They loved it. Some of their friends backed off, but a few came down. Some didn't last, but most found a way to get through it—at the back of the pack. Honestly, they didn't have a chance. After everything our players had gone through that summer, there was no way they were going to let some newbies win a single drill.

Even their friends who survived couldn't skate, so they couldn't help our team, but it still did us good to have them join us. Their suffering showed our guys just how far they'd come in just six weeks. For at least ninety minutes, three times a week, the former laughingstocks of the high school were now the kings of the hill.

Back when the University of Michigan still kept its football stadium, the nation's largest, open to the public, I decided to spice up our routine and test our limits by moving one of our workouts to the "Big House" to tackle the world's biggest Stairmaster, with 4,476 steps. (Yep, I once counted them all.)

By August 11, we had built up our conditioning and our confidence enough to believe we could do it. On a beautiful summer day, we gathered under the old press box, all of us a little nervous, chugging water and Gatorade and stretching out. When we were ready, we yelled at the top of our lungs, started the clock, and bolted out of the shade into the sunshine, down the steps to the fifty-yard line, then across the first row and up the next aisle in a long line of players pumping their legs up the stairs. We kept it up until we had gone around the entire stadium and back to the press box, in about fifteen minutes.

"[Coach] never failed to mention that it was the largest stadium in the country," Scooter McConnell remembers, "and since the only other high school in town wasn't doing it, by definition, we were running more steps than anyone in the country. A few people threw up their Gatorade, but everyone finished."

Hockey mom Robin Kunkel recalls showing up to photograph the event. "I was tired and hot on that summer day just watching them."

But we were thrilled. I no longer had to sell the hard, because they were reveling in it.

After we finished, I had a surprise for Mike Henry, whose leadership had been exemplary. I had his back, he had mine, and I wanted the whole team to know it. So after we finished, I told him to get on my back. Then I carried him up to the press box.

"That was us working hard and having fun," Henry says today. "That's what I wanted all along. We were on the same page by then — but I weighed 180 pounds and you weighed 160, so I thought you were going to drop me down the steps."

I didn't drop him. I didn't blow out my knees. I *ran* Captain Henry sixty rows up to the press box, and a tradition was born: the Captain Carry.

I'd assumed that transforming one of the softest high school hockey teams into one of the toughest in two short months might create some attrition. I certainly didn't want anyone to drop out, but I'd have been foolish not to anticipate that some might, especially since we weren't talking about a bunch of self-selected go-getters, but the same players who had finished 0-22-3, last of the nation's one thousand teams. Many had considered quitting even before we started working out — the same guys everyone kept telling me were hopeless.

But by the time we capped eight weeks of hard work with our last summer workout, on Friday, August 18, *not one single player had quit!* We had become a lean, mean, stretching, counting, lifting, running, and wall-sitting *machine.*

More proof of how much we'd changed in just two months came from Rod Sorge, our trainer. Before we started our last summer workout — in which we'd be running 220-yard relays on our school track for almost forty-five minutes, a brutal test against the clock — I'd asked Sorge for a large water jug and a stack of paper cups. When he dropped them off at the weight room, he saw everyone stretching and counting — loud and sharp, all player-driven, with captain Henry leading the way — exactly what I'd wanted to see at our first workout, when we couldn't do any of those things. Sorge was so shocked that he quietly returned to his training room to fetch his student trainers and brought them back to watch us through the doorway, amazed. The change was that dramatic.

Then we ran out to the track, yelling and screaming the whole way, completely jacked up to run our relays. On their last summer workout the players figured out that if the faster runners waited for the slower runners, we could cut our team's time down even more — and they did, smashing all our previous records. They had never impressed me more.

"To right our ship, we knew it wasn't going to be easy," Elmo recalls, "but I don't think we knew what not being terrible actually entailed: blistering hot workouts on the track and in the weight room. But hey, 'This is Huron, and it's harder over here.' By the end of the summer, we weren't a bunch of individuals, but a band of brothers."

That apparently included the coaches. Around that time Elmo told one parent, "At first I hated that guy's guts," referring to me, "but now I really like him."

When we jogged back to the gym that day, triumphant, *every player* finished a five-minute wall-sit, like they'd been doing it their whole lives.

"Gentlemen, you did it," I told them. "You've just completed twenty-four killer workouts, *together*. When I started, *this* is what I'd envisioned. This is it! No other team just did what you did. *No one else! You* are now the hardest-working hockey team in the state, no question — and *it's not even close!*

"This summer, we got better. A lot better. Now let's see what we can do."

They left that day with an unprecedented level of pride, and they'd earned it.

"By our last workout," Henry recalls, "the 'too cool to care' culture had already changed. We didn't care if it was cool to care anymore. *We cared.* That's when the team bought in. Now we know how to do the little things right, so we can start moving on to bigger things."

We hadn't won a game yet, and there was no guarantee we would. As of that day, our record still stood at 0-22-3, the nation's worst. But by the end of August, the Huron River Rats had taken the first crucial step: they were putting themselves on the line.

I often quoted Vince Lombardi's great line: "The harder we work, the harder it is to surrender." To which I added: *"And the bigger we can dream."*

By the end of our first summer, no one was surrendering, and they were daring to dream — talking openly about our first regular-season game, and even memorizing the date: November 18, exactly three months later.

- As a leader, if you're living in fear of being fired, you'll make too many compromises, your people will quit believing in you, and because of that, you could get fired anyway. You might as well do what you think is right. It's the *only* way to reach your potential.

- No person in your organization is more important than the team and its principles — including you. There are no "irreplaceable people," but your principles must hold.

- When your people start sharing your team's philosophy with each other, it becomes self-perpetuating — and now you have a real culture.

- The harder you work, the harder it is to surrender and the bigger you can dream. Without hard work, grit, and belief, no theory, strategy, or tactic will save you. But *with* hard work, grit, and belief, anything's possible. Don't apologize for hard work. *Celebrate it!*

4

Make Sure You're the
Dumbest Guy in the Room

- You don't need to be the smartest person in the room.
  You just need to figure out who is.

- Trying someone out beats résumés and interviews.
  Hire slower, fire faster.

- Hire people who are loyal, but strong enough to disagree.

Once you're in charge, one of your first and most vital tasks is to build your staff. Get this right, and you solve a lot of problems before they start, and you can set your sights much higher. Get this wrong, and you'll be spending your time cleaning up everyone else's messes instead of getting your own work done. You'll have to cut back on your plans — and with them, your dreams.

Given its obvious importance, I'm struck by how many organizations hire their people so poorly. Posting a job notice online, sorting through résumés for key words, and conducting a few superficial interviews will not get you what you want — but by then you're stuck with whoever shows up.

I learned a lot from my second job out of college, which entailed interviewing five hundred college seniors around the country for teaching jobs in private schools. It showed me how worthless the conventional hiring process really is. It took me all of two weeks to drop the dumb question, "What are your strengths and weaknesses?" Their strengths were countless: "I'm a hard worker," "I'm a great team player," and "I like working with people!" And their sole weakness? "I care too much," or "I'm a perfectionist!"

I would have paid good money to hear just one candidate say, "Weaknesses? Let's see: I like to show up late, take long lunches, and leave early. Oh, and I tend to undermine authority. How's that?"

"You're hired!"

Whenever I ask my audiences if they've ever been fooled by a résumé and an interview, every hand goes up. Then I ask them how hard it is to get rid of someone who fooled them. The groans are audible. Firing an employee these days can take one year's time and salary, not to mention the hidden costs in turnover and morale.

Dismissing people who clearly can't do the job or who behave inappropriately is expensive. But unlike employees who steal, drink in the office, or harass coworkers, mediocrities are often much tougher to eradicate and can burden you for years.

That's why it's a bad idea to fill even an urgent personnel need with the nearest warm body. Ari Weinzweig, cofounder of Ann Arbor's famed Zingerman's Delicatessen, told me they learned the hard way in filling positions at their fourteen stores that no matter how desperate they are, simply hiring anyone off the street almost always backfires. Unqualified people will create problems that experienced workers have to fix, and their mere presence will force your capable employees to conclude that you must not think too highly of what they do if you hire as though anyone can do it.

No, you want people who are passionate about your organization and the kind of work they'll be doing for you. If you don't find that, *keep looking until you do*. Yes, this approach requires more time, energy, thought, and money than the typical process. But it still costs far less than getting rid of someone who fooled you.

So, unless the position you're seeking to fill consists entirely of writing fancy résumés and charming interviewers, don't rely on those tools to find your people.

In contrast, the best organizations I've worked with, reported on, and researched, including the New York Yankees, Cirque du Soleil, the Navy SEALS, Menlo Innovations, and Zingerman's, all utilize tryout periods when candidates do the actual work for at least a month or two. I realize that not all organizations can do this, but I believe most can if they're willing to get creative. I do know that trying someone out is the only way you can be sure there's a good fit. Résumés and interviews, which often have built-in biases, are quickly eclipsed by actual on-the-job performance.

Don't tell me who you are. *Show me.*

The first thing I did after Rod Sorge told me that I would be the River Rats' next hockey coach was to send out a clarion call for help. I was only thirty-five years old, but I'd been playing hockey for almost three decades, so I knew lots of hockey people around town.

But what did I have to offer? A sweat suit, a pair of hockey gloves, and a baseball cap in exchange for hard, inconvenient hours turning around a bottom-feeder. How many adults can commit to working from 3 p.m. to 6 p.m. four days a week, then hop on a bus for games on Wednesday and Saturday nights? If I had posted this position online, I'd probably have gotten a lot more laughs than takers.

The key, once again, was relationships. Everyone always says, "It's a small world!," but let me add the punch line: "It's a small world — so don't be a jackass." I liked to think that in my thirty-five years I had not been a jackass too often — though I'm sure plenty might have disagreed, and they probably had receipts. But whatever good karma I had built up over my life to that point, now was the time to cash it in.

I did not conduct one formal interview or solicit a single résumé. I just asked some hockey friends I admired, respected, and trusted if they wanted to help out. I didn't sugarcoat the fact that our mission was going to be difficult and the compensation was – well, virtually nonexistent.

Amazingly, a dozen friends, acquaintances, and friends of friends showed up at some point during our preseason practices. This proves another important point: *employees recruit employees.* So you better hire good ones. Hard workers know other hard workers, smart people know smart people, and good people know good people. Likewise, lazy, stupid jerks tend to hang out with lazy, stupid jerks. So if you hire good workers, you'll find more good workers. If you hire lazy, stupid jerks – well, be prepared to see their friends apply.

Companies could save a good chunk of their recruitment budget if they just treated their people better. This dramatically reduces turnover and makes recruitment easier because happy employees urge their friends to apply.

I didn't have to weed anyone out, because they made their own decisions before tryouts. In most cases, the time commitment was too much. Others may not have agreed with my vision, or didn't think I had one, or weren't too keen on taking direction from someone who couldn't play as well as they could. I don't know.

I did know that the seven guys who stuck with me and the players were going to be great coaches *because they already were great coaches.* And I knew that because we'd been working together for four months. I knew what each one could contribute, and they knew what kind of program I wanted to run. There would be no bait-and-switches on either side, no surprises, no "Wish I would've known!" They were so good that I'm confident that I could have turned the program over to any one of them and we wouldn't have missed a beat.

Although most high school hockey teams had two assistants, what reason did I have not to keep all seven? They were all hardworking, smart, honest, and fun, but each offered something special on top of all that. Rob Brown had played forward for Michigan and pro hockey in Sweden. Jef Forward and Pete Uher were probably the two best defensemen in our senior league. We also had two excellent goalie coaches — because you can never have too much help for the most important position in team sports — and a "bonus coach" in athletic trainer Rod Sorge. To this day I don't know if Rod can skate, but I do know he has an uncanny knack for taking the pulse of a team. I frequently relied on his insights.

"You knew what you didn't know and sought the right help," goalie Steve Beltran recalls. "You had a nice mix of really talented hockey players and some puck-pushers that complemented each other. They knew how to have fun and work hard."

Their day jobs included running a custom cement company, starting an architectural firm, and getting an MBA, but they still made time — even if getting to practice required a forty-minute dash from Ford World Headquarters. Initially they might have come down as a favor to me, but they stayed because the players drew them in. The assistants were not just overqualified — they could really connect.

"That's the problem with work today," says former captain-turned–Insight Global vice president Stevie Wasik. "Everyone is so smart, they forget their people are human beings first. At Huron we had a room full of coaches who cared about us, and we would do anything for them. I have built my entire career on that principle."

The relationship between the assistants and the players was vital. If you're the leader, you're automatically the bad cop — like it or not. When the boom needs to come down, it has to come from *you*, not from one of your lieutenants.

By midseason every year, I could identify each player's favorite coach — and it frequently wasn't me. No problem. When a player had a concern, what an advantage it was to have an assistant who could talk with him in confidence, or simply bring him under his wing. The assistants would often learn of the players' problems before I did because some of the players felt more comfortable talking with them.

Scooter McConnell recalls, "We knew the new coaching staff at the beginning of our first season better than we had known the previous one at the end of the last."

Two coaches in particular underscored the value of hiring this way: our oldest coach, and our youngest. Ned Glysson, a biochemist who led a company that produced cellular concrete, had been running our adult league team, Zell, for fifteen years. Most of the coaches played for Zell, which won the A-league title as often as not, but what really impressed us was *how* Ned did it.

When a former University of Michigan player who'd won two NCAA titles asked to play for Zell, any other beer league coach would have said, "Great! Sign him up!" But not Coach Ned, who asked, "What kind of guy is he?" And that's the kind of guy Ned is.

Coach Ned was the only assistant who was older than I was, had already been a head coach, was married, or had kids. He was also an Eagle Scout, fer cryin' out loud, who taught Sunday school for fifteen years. Ned provided a lot of valuable perspectives.

At the other end of the age spectrum we had Mike Lapprich, aka Lapper, whom I first met when I was an assistant and he was just a ninth-grader—an oversized puppy. When I became Huron's head coach five years later, Lapper had just finished his second year as an assistant at the ripe age of nineteen. I learned later that he was supposed to get half the assistant coach's pay that year—about $1,500—but he never got a dime.

"Nobody would have blamed Lapp if he'd said, 'To hell with this,' and moved on," Scooter McConnell recalls. "It says a lot about him that he came back anyway. Maybe because Lapp was only a few years older, he was really one part coach, one part mentor, and one part friend. He had a fun-loving spirit, but he showed us how to conduct ourselves, how to be a good teammate, and how to treat others at all times."

Whenever someone felt like quitting that first summer, Lapper kept them going.

"Henry, Elmo, and I were just talking about how smart it was to keep Lapper on the coaching staff," Beltran told me recently. "He had few coaching credentials, but he helped us buy in to you and your system, the perfect middle man. Not the most talented hockey player on your staff, compared to the college and pro players, but definitely the most valuable."

"If you were the face of the team," Elmo says, "Lapp was the heart."

At the end of our first summer together, our athletic director asked me to pick one official assistant coach who would get the $3,000 salary. Frankly, if I had relied on interviews and résumés, I doubt I would have picked Lapper — and that would have been a big loss for everyone. But because I'd seen how Lapper worked with our people at every single workout and practice, that was the easiest decision I had to make.

"Mike Lapprich," I told her.

She looked up. "He just turned twenty? Are you *sure?*"

"Trust me," I said. "I'm sure."

Two months after my lunch with Mike Henry, I could see he was right.

The coaches met before and after all practices and games in the small coaches' room, where there was no place to hide.

I'm sure I was not always charming to work with, especially our first year. I was often short-fused; distracted, with a million things spinning in my head; trying to talk to three people at once; laser-focused on a particular task, oblivious to all else; or simply too insecure about my own authority, while trying to win a hockey game or two, to listen like I should have. But that's exactly why I needed strong assistants to push back.

Like gum magnate William Wrigley Jr. said, "When two business partners always agree, one of them is unnecessary." By that measure, suffice it to say, we were all necessary.

If I said something stupid, they'd usually just look at me, disappointed, and that was all it took for me to apologize or shut up, such was my respect for their judgment. When I was going astray, they'd give me a nudge.

"You were pretty tough on Sam."

"You sure you want to do that?"

"Nick's been making progress. I think you should look at him again."

I expected the assistants to be both honest and loyal. "You can say whatever you want to me in the coaches' room," I told them. "But once we walk out this door, I'm still the head coach. That means no undermining me with the players, the parents, or my boss. You want to disagree, you can do it here."

They never once broke my rule. Their loyalty was rock-solid — and I certainly hope I returned it. At our team meeting every year, I told the players, if they had a problem, a question, or an idea, they could bring it to me or another coach. But if they backtalked to me, that was one problem. If they backtalked to one of the assistants, they'd have every problem in the world.

"I will take their side," I said, "every single time."

As usual, I meant it.

Too often leaders confuse loyalty with blind obedience, and they value it so highly because they don't want to be challenged. They hire weak staffers who are little more than yes-people: they can't lead by definition, because they are incapable of taking the initiative, and therefore they're of no real use. Loyalty from weak assistants doesn't count for much. So don't make the same deal with the devil I see too many leaders make: if you don't challenge me, I won't challenge you. Sign that pact and you may get peace, but you'll never get real success.

Strong assistants also help you make informed decisions. We had only ten minutes between periods while the Zamboni cleaned the ice to figure out what was working and what wasn't, and what to tell the players to do about it. Our assistants saw things I didn't and saved me from my blind spots, my biases, and my dumbest ideas. Even better, they gave me their best ideas — if I was smart enough to take them.

Entering that first season, our comfort level with each other was extremely high, and the unknowns among us very few. Whatever was going to happen that season, I had complete confidence that I had filled the coaches' room with the very best people available, and the players agreed. Name just about any measure that mattered — knowledge of the game, defense, the parents, the players — and I finished no higher than second among our coaches. But I did do the one thing that only I could do: I hired a great staff. If you're trying to rebuild your airplane in midair, it really helps if everyone onboard is an aeronautical engineer.

At our first parents' meeting, I said, "My goal was to be the dumbest guy in the coaches' room — and I've greatly exceeded my expectations."

Contrary to the CEO-as-Superman myth, you don't have to be the smartest guy in the room. I think it might even be a disadvantage — not that I'd know. But you *do* have to recognize who's smarter, get them on your team, and let them do their jobs.

I took a similar approach to selecting the players, although there were some important differences. State rules prohibited us from recruiting anyone; we couldn't even recruit players who were already attending Huron but played for outside travel teams. Our first year we didn't have an abundance of players to choose from either. But none of that stopped us from picking the players the same way I picked the coaches: through a long process designed to determine which players could really do the work we wanted them to do and were excited about doing it.

First, I don't buy it when organizations say, "If we don't lower our standards, we'll never get enough candidates." If someone can't do the job you need them to do, how does it help to hire them to do that job poorly? *You do not need them all.*

Second, your standards — for behavior more than performance — must be more important than the size of the talent pool. Start relaxing your standards to meet the lowest common denominator and you'll sacrifice both your standards *and* your talent pool. But if you uphold your high standards, your candidate pool will grow—and with people who can actually do the work.

In its heyday Borders Books practiced this approach to great effect. Brothers Tom and Louis Borders founded Borders Books in Ann Arbor in 1971 and built it into an international empire with 1,249 stores worldwide. Borders provided decent pay and health care, but that's not why overqualified graduate students wanted to work there.

When I was a college junior I asked for an application. They handed me a literature test I had to take on the spot. It was brutal. Despite studying history and English, I didn't pass. But that meant the people who worked there *had* passed the test, and you had to respect that. They certainly respected themselves and felt special to be working there—even for ten bucks an hour. The key? Borders didn't *apologize* for its high standards but *reveled* in them—and that made it special to work there.

Building a special place to work takes years, but it isn't a permanent state of mind. Far from it. In 1989, Borders dropped the literature test, which disappointed the veterans and attracted less passionate employees. That didn't sink the company, but it didn't help. New leaders, bigger mistakes, bad timing, and bad luck resulted in the bankruptcy in 2011—but it started with dropping the test.

At the end of our first summer, Steve Sheldon, the same parent who had voted for me during the interview process, asked me if we wanted to join an informal, eleven-game fall league. I'd given this no thought, but after discussing it with the assistants, we saw an opportunity to evaluate our progress through a better lens.

State rules mandated that no paid coaches could participate, so I asked Coach Ned, the Zell men's league coach, and Billy Tucker, a star from Huron's 1994 team, if they'd be willing to serve as the bench coaches. They not only said yes, they showed up for all the games wearing dress shirts and sport coats. That sent a message too.

The league wasn't nearly as tough as our winter league would be, but our guys gained confidence, won some games, and had a chance to show the coaches watching from the stands how they played under game pressure. This was very valuable, because some players look great in tryouts, then get beat by the grinders in the playoffs, when it matters most.

I didn't want show horses. I wanted workhorses. Give me a grinder any day. You don't find them through résumés and interviews. You find them by putting them to work.

I also wanted players who wanted to play for us. I realize that sounds silly, but managers spend a lot of time chasing people who really don't want to work with them. Begging someone to work for you is as ill advised as begging someone to marry you.

Worst-case scenario: they say yes.

- **Résumés and interviews don't tell you much. The best way to find out if people can do the job is to have them do the job. The best-run companies use trial periods before making a hiring decision. You should too.**

- **You don't have to be the smartest guy in the room. But you do need to figure out who is, hire them, and let them do their job.**

- **Instead of hiring yes-people, find those who are strong enough to question you when needed. They'll give you their best work, and real loyalty.**

- **Remember, once you become the leader, you're the bad cop. If your people like your assistants more than you, congratulations. You hired well.**

5

Reduce Your Rules,
but Make Them Stick

- Make your rules clear, few, and connected to your larger mission.

- Make sure your rules are within everyone's control to follow every day.

- When your people start enforcing the rules themselves, *the culture has changed.*

Nobody likes a lot of rules, especially pointless or counterproductive ones. I've found that younger people have even less tolerance for useless rules than older folks. So how do you pare your list down to the essentials?

Let's start with this: never make rules you won't enforce. If you're not willing to back them up with consistent consequences, then you don't have rules they will respect, follow, and ultimately internalize.

For example, some high school teams have "zero tolerance" policies for underage drinking. Lovely idea perhaps, but how do you plan on enforcing that? By driving around town barging into people's homes, searching open fields to spy on teenagers' parties, and breaking into barns to see who might be drinking? If you catch some of them, are you prepared to kick them off your team with no second chances? What happens then? Won't they just drink *more?* What about the kids who happen to drink somewhere else and don't get caught? Do they get off scot-free?

I don't like any of that. I had some serious rules on drinking, but they boiled down to this: the responsibility is on you to handle yourselves, not on me to catch you. If an alcohol issue ends up on my desk, that means you can't handle it, and you won't like my solution. I guarantee it will be harsher than the school's.

I could have just followed the Boston Celtics' legendary coach and general manager Red Auerbach, who had one rule: "Don't do anything to embarrass yourself, or the Celtics."

Honestly, what else do you need?

My ultimate goal was not to create a long list of rules and punishments, but to establish clear expectations and a shared sense of purpose to get them to internalize our principles. If I could do that, I thought, a thick rulebook wouldn't be necessary because our players would internalize our guiding principles and *take pride in them.* I wanted them to know what we expected them to do and not to do, and why we did things the way we did, so they would believe in our philosophy so deeply that they would pass those guidelines on to the others.

I wasn't sure how I was going to do all that until I came across a note I'd made for myself months before, when the Huron coaching position had just opened up. I'd been walking out of Michigan's Yost Arena after we'd finished our weekly pickup game with the Michigan alumni hockey players, a fast bunch I was lucky to join. That night I happened to be walking out with Rob Palmer, the assistant captain of Michigan's 1977 NCAA runner-up team and a former NHL player. He said his dad always told him, "Just focus on two things: *work hard, and support your teammates.*"

I wrote that down when I got home, and I saw the note again when I was preparing my first letter to the team. The more I thought about it the more convinced I became that those two points alone could serve as our guiding principles. Who could argue with either one? Who could say those expectations were unimportant, unreasonable, meaningless, or too hard to understand or execute? Could anyone claim that abiding by these principles was out of their control or subject to dumb luck, the referees, or the weather?

No, you can decide to work hard and support your teammates every day you wake up. No one can stop you from doing them, and both will have a serious impact on your team.

This sets up an important point: it's crucial that you and your team focus intensely on *what you send out* to the world, and *not on what comes back.*

We didn't have much control over the latter, especially that first year – the wins and losses, our ranking, or whether our opponents were going to schedule us for an easy win on Parents Night, Senior Night, or whenever they wanted to play their backup goalie. But from day one we had *complete control* over what we were putting out there: working hard and supporting our teammates.

This is something I learned when I was twenty-four, my first year as a freelance writer: work like hell to make sure the articles I submitted to magazine editors were the absolute best I could write, but then forget about them once I dropped them in the mail, then go back to work on the next ones. I didn't control whatever the editors sent back – whether it was a freelance contract or, more likely, a rejection – and therefore I couldn't waste my energy thinking about it too much. I figured if I just kept doing everything I could to send out better articles, the rest would eventually take care of itself. I applied the same approach to coaching Huron.

"We couldn't control what other teams did," Scooter McConnell recalls. "We couldn't control how much raw talent we had. But we could control how hard we worked. When you put your all into something, you tend to guard the gains you've made."

Taking this approach allowed us to *define ourselves completely,* instead of letting the world do it for us. We already knew how the world defined us: as a record-setting pack of losers. Did we really need to hear more of that? But if we decided to define ourselves solely by how well we fulfilled our two principles, work hard and support our teammates, whatever the world had to say about us — whether it was our opponents' disrespect, the local paper's stories, or the kids' snickering at school — *didn't matter.*

As they say, "What other people think of you is none of your business."

In our case, what other people thought of us was potentially lethal. If we sipped from that toxic swamp, we'd be dead before we got started. It was essential that we drowned out all that external negativity by defining ourselves with the steady drumbeat of our two principles.

With that in mind, I put up a sign in our locker room: EVERYTHING WE NEED TO WIN IS INSIDE THIS ROOM. Whatever was outside of it officially didn't matter to us.

Once we set up our two guiding principles, what else did we really need? Just about every rule you could think of for a high school hockey team — or a high-powered law firm or a world-class hospital or a first-rate company — fits neatly under one of those two principles, and often both. So instead of giving our team a hundred rules to follow, I presented those two principles prominently in my opening letter to them when I was named the head coach.

I didn't just send the letter and forget about it either — which is exactly what most companies do with their "shared values," "mission statements," and the like. If your employees can't recite them, let alone follow them, do they even exist?

No, we repeated our two principles endlessly all summer in the gym, on the track, and at the rink. I'd ask them: "What's the first rule of Huron hockey?"

"Work hard!"

"What is it?"

"Work hard!"

"What's the second rule of Huron hockey?"

"Support your teammates!"

"What is it?"

"Support your teammates!"

When we finally moved into our locker room in November, I printed our two principles in big letters on a sheet, laminated it, and stuck it to the coaches' room door, so that was the first thing everyone saw when they walked in. When you hear, read, and say your own rules enough times, you start living them. And when you start living them, they're not merely your rules — they're your *values*.

Yes, we had other rules too, but *everything* derived from our two rules or we didn't care about it.

Being on time, for example, was fair, logical, and utterly transparent. At 3 p.m., you were either inside the locker room, ready to work, or you weren't. It was also pretty obvious to everyone that, with only a few hours each day for two dozen players to work together, it was important for everyone to be on time. Being on time was a straightforward test, easily assessed, with real benefits for all.

Likewise, we expected them to show up dressed appropriately — whether in their "grays" (T-shirt and shorts) for indoor workouts, their "blacks" (fleece sweat suits) for outdoor workouts, or green shirts and gold ties for game nights — and on time, every time. "Five o'clock means five o'clock." We meant it.

If punctuality and attire matter to your organization — say, you expect your employees to wear collared shirts and start their Zoom sessions on time — then say so, without apology, but also explain why it's connected to your bigger mission.

It is absolutely imperative that whatever your rules, you enforce them with utter fairness. Your team needs to see this to trust you — and they'll be watching.

I put a lot of thought into our practices and took suggestions from the assistants and the players. I printed out three copies of the practice schedule every day, with an inspirational or funny quote at the bottom. I taped one copy on the wall they saw on the way into the locker room, one on the plexiglass of the scorekeeper's booth, and a third on the other side of the rink. The players would *always* take a look at what we had in store for them that day and cheer when they saw one of their favorite drills had made the list.

Lord knows I'm a talker, but I almost never stopped practice to talk on the ice. Hey, renting ice-time cost three bucks a minute! So I'd go over our practice on the whiteboard beforehand in our locker room and review practice afterward on the same board. On the ice, unless we were learning a new drill, or I wasn't happy with what I was seeing, all I had to do was blow the whistle and wave my stick to show them where to go next. They would start the following drill seconds later. They didn't need anything more. They were *sharp*.

I honestly didn't think this routine was a big deal until a lot of players brought it up when I asked them for help on this book. Why was it so important to them? Because the mere act of posting our schedule set the tone for so much of what we did. Corporations call it daily communication: letting everybody know what's expected of them that day. Turns out, employees want to know what's going on. That's a good thing.

"Every day," recalls Bobby Chappuis, now a general manager at Uber Freight, "we had an agenda taped on the glass at the rink, structured down to the minute. Whether or not we liked what was on the agenda, we knew what to expect. This gave the team clear expectations, but it also made the practice feel purposeful. We were there for a reason, and those agendas reinforced that idea."

These principles trickled down to seemingly minor things too. For example, we used green tape on our green "away" socks and white tape on our white "home" socks. (We supplied plenty of both, stacked in cool pyramids on the training table, just like the pros.) If someone, usually a rookie, started putting white tape on his green socks, I could just look at him, then his socks, make an expression, and ask if we might have a senior handy who could help this wayward soul dress himself. The seniors were always happy to help.

We didn't do all those things to satisfy some fetish with rules or

agendas or attire. We did them because they promoted our principles, they reflected our values, and they helped us define ourselves.
Shortly into our first winter season, those things were no longer a
chore. They had become *cool*.

Not long after our first team meeting on Henry's back deck, when I
chewed them out for not turning in their questionnaires, it became
extremely rare to see anyone show up late for anything. But in our
first few weeks it did happen occasionally, and when it did, instead
of calculating some arbitrary punishment, I'd look at the offender
and give one of our stock responses, at varying levels of humor:

"Ah, lovely to see you, Billy. Got a watch? Need a new one?"

"Oh, I forgot. Rick: can you tell me when our workout starts?"

"Can you think of any reason why Ramsey needs to be on time,
but you don't?"

And then the closer: "What's the first rule of Huron hockey?"

"Work hard."

"What is it?" I'd say, turning to the team.

"Work hard!"

Then I'd ask the offender. "Does that include getting here on
time?"

"Yes, it does."

"Right. What's the second rule?"

"Support your teammates," he'd mumble.

"What is it?" I'd ask the team.

"Support your teammates!"

I'd ask the offender: "Do you agree with that?"

"Yes, Coach."

I'd nod. "Then you have a chance to prove it next time. And you
can prove it right now by jumping into our stretching and help everyone get going."

Once our first winter season started, I bought an "atomic clock,"
which claimed to be perfectly accurate because it bounced off satel-

lites and involved atoms somehow and — okay, it doesn't make much sense to me either. But it really was scarily accurate, and it became a running joke: "Is your watch atomic? No? Okay, then we'll go by this one on the wall." Making the atomic clock the only timepiece that mattered kept things simple and ended a lot of arguments.

If you were late for a winter practice or a game, you wouldn't play the next game. I made it severe enough that I rarely had to use it. I didn't want to, because punishing people is a waste of time.

"The kids were surprised at first that we would hold them accountable," assistant coach Pete Uher recalls, "even if they had an excuse. Then they started to demand accountability of each other."

I knew this was sinking in our first fall when one of my old neighbors, a dental hygienist, told me one of my players had warned her that he had to leave at 11:30 sharp to make our noon workout. "Early is on time," he had told her, "and on time is late, and we can't be late." Progress!

During our four years together, thirty players arrived at the locker room before more than one hundred games, and four hundred practices. Not counting our off-season games and practices, that's still fifteen thousand chances to be late. Yet only five players, or 0.0003 percent, were even a second late, and they didn't bother whining or giving me lame excuses. They came to me hat in hand to apologize profusely. I never had to say much, because they already felt worse about sitting out the next game than I did.

It didn't take long to reduce all this to shorthand. If a player was late, not wearing the right clothes, or missing a piece of equipment, all I had to do was look at them, in front of the whole team, and ask, "What's the first rule?" The question alone was enough.

After a few months, I had complete confidence that anyone who showed up a minute late and got the two-rules treatment wasn't going to be late again the rest of the season. Even better, the two rules became so ingrained that I didn't even have to bring them up. The players, especially the captains and seniors, did it for me — or really, for themselves and the team they were now leading.

They were soon enforcing our rules themselves. If a high school hockey team can do that, your company can too. Think how many problems that would solve.

Being strict on our two rules allowed us to be loose about other things. I cared about what I cared about 100 percent. I did not care about anything else. If you squeeze the balloon on all sides at once, it pops. You can't have a hundred rules with no outlet for your people to relax.

In business this is called "loose-tight management," and it works with high school hockey teams, university classes, and major corporations. Loose-tight management increases your odds of getting full cooperation with what you care about, avoids a leaders-versus-labor dynamic, and prevents your people from burning out.

In our case, that meant I officially didn't care about profanity in our locker room, on our bench, or on the ice. Truth is, I was a practitioner myself. As one player told his father, "Coach swears more when he's happy than you do when you're mad." I can say my swearing was never misogynistic, homophobic, or directed at anyone — but I still can't defend it. Nonetheless, I didn't care if they swore privately among themselves, so long as they didn't do it in public, in front of people not on our team.

The locker room was their sanctuary, so I didn't care about the music they played there, how loud they played it, or what they did until we started our routines. They played all kinds of music at top volume, some of it profane. I hated some of it, said so often, and freely made fun of it. But I never asked them to turn it down or off until it was time to get to work, and even then I rarely had to ask because the seniors took care of it themselves. In other words, I treated them like adults.

If you pick just a few rules that make sense, are tied to your greater mission, and can be enforced by others who also believe in them, then the rules become *theirs*, your culture is internalized, and everyone feels a part of it. With that, you've successfully swapped "you against them" into "us against the world."

And that's when things start getting fun.

Of course, any rule you have will be tested, and if it doesn't hold up, you're better off with no rule at all — just one more reason to keep the list as short as possible.

The first big test for our two rules came during our unofficial fall season, with Coach Ned and Billy Tucker leading the squad. We would play eleven games against small-town teams, a couple notches below the Michigan Metro League. But we hadn't beaten any of them in years, and we'd be playing a few that winter, when it counted.

That's why we were so eager to win our first fall game, which happened to be the night before our annual golf outing fundraiser. I wanted the guys to see that all of their hard work had paid off, and to have something positive to talk about the next morning.

No luck. We lost, 2–1.

But then we won a couple of games and tied Chelsea, a former farm town just outside Ann Arbor, twice. This bothered me because, although Chelsea had become a solid program, it didn't even have a hockey team when I played, and yet we couldn't beat them. Nothing stuck in my craw more that fall than our two ties against Chelsea.

A few weeks later, we had five wins, two losses, and two ties going into our third and final fall league matchup against — you guessed it — Chelsea. If we couldn't beat these guys after four months of hard work, I figured, we'd be in for a rough ride in the Metro League that winter, so this was something of a "statement game." It would also be played in Ann Arbor on a Saturday, so our players recruited their friends to cheer them on.

Unfortunately, I'd be traveling that night, October 21, to research a possible book on Title IX. During my flight, I wasn't thinking about the work ahead of me, but about the fall league hockey game being played behind me. When I got off the plane, I was so eager to hear if we'd finally beaten Chelsea that I made a beeline for the nearest pay phone. (Remember, this was 2000.) My machine had a dozen messages. That seemed odd, since I'd left home only two hours earlier.

"We talked to them before the game," Coach Ned's message said, "about the fans coming, and playing with their heads. We said you weren't here, so be on your best behavior. The players said the same thing. The game just ended. The game was called for a brawl. Seven guys suspended from each team, everyone on the ice."

My blood pressure soared — but at least I understood why I had a dozen messages.

The messages left by Coach Ned and many of the players — including Mike Henry, notably — told me the game had attracted a hundred classmates. Hardly a packed house, but unheard of for a fall league game, which added some energy to the night.

"It was a great game to watch from a hockey perspective," Coach Ned said.

But in the third period, with the score tied 1–1, Mike Henry dumped a Chelsea player near the Huron bench. When Henry skated away, the Chelsea player chased after him and jammed his stick between Henry's legs. Henry immediately turned and started swinging, but got knocked down from behind. Three Chelsea players piled on top of Henry, prompting fellow Huron senior Jake Ramsey to jump in to help him. And in a flash, every player on the ice paired off with an opponent and started fighting. (Fortunately, with modern equipment, it's almost impossible to hurt anyone in a high school hockey fight, and no one was injured.) When the dust settled, the refs wisely ended the game and sent both teams back to their locker rooms.

"I apologize," Coach Ned said into my machine. "I did everything I could."

When our guys got back to their locker room, they went nuts — screaming, yelling, high-fiving, and hugging.

"With all the fans and the testosterone," Coach Ned added, "I don't think I've ever seen them so fired up, even after a win. Maybe it'll help their chemistry in the long run. Hopefully the lesson will be learned, and something good can come out of this."

The players thought so.

Former senior Dave McMurtrie recalls, "The fact that we cared enough to fight for one another was a positive step compared to years past."

"We were so excited after that game," remembers Beltran, who was in the stands because he'd broken his ankle playing soccer that week. "Well, at least for a little while. I remember that excitement turning to fear when we realized that you had no idea what had happened. You seemed so strict at the time that some of the guys worried you might start kicking kids off the team."

But not captain Mike Henry.

"Personally, I was not concerned," he recalls. "Don't get me wrong. I knew it was bad, and we couldn't go around fighting everyone. We knew you were going to say something, and we were going to hear about it. We expected that.

"But I wasn't worried about you kicking guys off the team because I knew you well enough by then to know that once you heard what really happened, the whole story, it was going to be okay. So when everyone was freaking out about what you were going to do, I told them, 'Don't worry about it, guys. It's gonna be all right.' They fed off that, because they had confidence in our relationship. Three months earlier, I would have been nervous. Not then. We had a connection."

In hindsight, it was probably a lucky break for everyone, including me, that I was out of town. It gave us all more time and space to think about what had just happened, and what we should do about it. After I'd heard all the messages, my first thought was: *This is worse than a shellacking.* The melee represented the opposite of everything we were trying to be.

But after a long talk with Coach Ned, whose judgment I trusted completely, and some of the players, who were contrite, I started to see things a little differently. Yes, I fully supported the suspensions they'd be getting, and I planned to give them a stern lecture when I got back. I took it as a good sign that they already knew that was coming.

But if we were serious about our two rules, I had to assess how we'd done on that basis alone. By all accounts, they'd skated hard all night, but part of "working hard" is being disciplined, staying out of the penalty box, and steering clear of the stupidity that can quickly bubble up in a high school hockey game. So on our first principle I gave them a "C."

When it came to "support your teammates," it mattered that Jake Ramsey rushed to help Mike Henry, and the other players stood up for each other. Not the way I had envisioned, of course, but in the heat of the moment, how many options did they have? Did I expect them to stand there while three opponents pummeled their captain?

The locker-room celebration was unseemly, but it was fueled not by hooliganism, but by their excitement over making a statement: *they cared about each other*, and they would defend each other. If we were serious that "support your teammates" was one of our two principles, well, they'd done it, in spades. I had to give them an "A."

The more I thought about it, the more I realized this crazy fight was less indicative of things going desperately wrong than of some things going right. Our two principles might have gone through a little hell that night, but they had emerged the better for it, and so had our players.

Assistant coach Jef Forward, who also missed the game, captured this odd mix perfectly with his message: "Just got the news. A brawl! The boys are after my own heart. Of course I'd never tell 'em that, or condone that behavior. I know what your response is and should be. But I've got a big smile on my face. They're playing with *heart*. Maybe the only positive, but a big positive. Make sure you make them come to the games they're forced to sit out. Can we field a team for Wednesday's game?!?"

When he ended with a chuckle, I couldn't resist finally cracking a grin.

Four days later, I met with the seven suspended players under the stands a few minutes before our last fall league game. To their credit, they didn't have to be told to show up well in advance. They didn't want to add any fuel to the fire. After I asked them what had happened and they repeated what I already knew — without excuses — I asked them to predict my reaction. They hit all the right notes: disappointed, frustrated, upset.

I underscored the obvious, in a tone that was serious but calm: "We're not the kind of team that engages in bench-clearing brawls. We're here to play hockey. *This is never going to happen again.* And I know you understand that."

They nodded solemnly. This was crucial. If they hadn't understood the seriousness of the situation, I could never have said what I said next. After letting it all sink in for a beat or two, I added, "But I also have to say, I'm proud that you stood up for each other. I can't say it's how I wanted to see it, but I can say you supported your teammates. This team has a real bond. We'll learn how to channel this, but we're going to be okay.

"I know you're not playing tonight, but be sure to give your teammates on the ice all the support you can. They're going to need it."

The suspended players and some of the coaches watched our last fall league game together in the stands. With only ten players in uniform going against Dexter's full twenty, I expected a butt-kicking, a big step backward right before our tryouts, which would make plain the price we were paying for that fight.

But their understudies played *inspired* hockey, dominating a game they had no business being in. They won a jaw-dropper, 6–0, while taking only a few minor penalties. The suspended players cheered every hit, every shot, and every goal. They were proud of their teammates — and probably relieved their friends on the ice were mitigating the damage done by the suspensions.

After the game the suspended players, unprompted by me, went down to congratulate the guys as they came off the ice and then celebrated together in the locker room. And *that* is exactly what I was looking for.

They were not only becoming a team — they were starting to lead themselves.

Saturday, November 18. After tryouts whittled our team down to twenty-five varsity and seven reserve players, the date we'd been shouting for months during our workouts had finally arrived. We were going to play our first official winter game against Grand Ledge Waverly, a team that had whitewashed Huron the year before, 5–0.

Before that game I played a little trick on our guys. Our new home jerseys — which the seniors had designed on Henry's back deck — had just come in; they looked fantastic, and I knew the guys would love them. But I told them their jerseys wouldn't be ready in time. They were deeply disappointed when they had to put on their old, ugly game jerseys and head out for warm-ups. But once they left the locker room, we hung up their new jerseys in each player's stall so when they returned from warm-ups that was the first thing they saw.

"Ohhh, man!"

"Look at these!"

"Awesome!"

"Little things like switching the jerseys after warm-ups had such an impact," Jake Ramsey recalls. "When you've struggled for a whole season and you don't feel like people have any faith in your team, the most trivial thing can absolutely ignite a team — and that's exactly what happened."

We came out strong but fell behind 1–0. The guys tied it up 1–1 a few minutes later, then their conditioning took over in the last two periods to produce five unanswered goals.

Final score: 6–1. First win in more than a year.

I turned to the assistants, shook their hands, and said, "Thank God that's over with." Then we saw the players mobbing our goalie like they'd won the Stanley Cup.

"I specifically remember you asking me, 'What the hell is going on?'" Jake Ramsey says. "I said, 'Coach, we haven't had anything to celebrate in over a year!'"

When we walked off the ice, we saw the parents — we had no other fans then — standing, clapping, and *crying*. They kept cheering for their boys long after the game had ended.

I turned to Coach Ned and said, "Last year must've been worse than we imagined."

We won our next game, 2–0, our first shutout in three years. I asked Henry to talk to the reporter who was covering the game, and he sounded like a veteran coach: "We just all stuck together and played together as a team. We all played our hearts out."

We played our third game "downriver" — in the blue-collar Detroit suburbs — against one of the weaker Metro League teams, but still the best team we'd played so far. For years the Rats had been everyone's favorite opponent for Parents Night, Senior Night, and yes, Backup Goalie Night. But with their second-string goalie in net, we stunned them by jumping out to a 3–0 lead. They put their starting goalie back in and closed the gap to 3–2, but we held on to mark our first Metro League win in three years.

Our guys still remember the bus ride home, with Mike Henry singing "How Sweet It Is, to Be 3-and-0," Dave McMurtrie and Mike "P-Love" Perry beat-boxing, and even yours truly rapping some Grand Master Flash and the Furious Five. It was a night to bask in, and we did.

"That week at school everyone knew our record," Scooter McConnell recalls. "Not because they loved hockey, but because we wouldn't shut up about it."

In our fourth game we came down to earth against one of the Metro League's better teams with an 8–3 loss. Then we faced the best Metro League team, Trenton, which would provide the second big test for our simple Two Rules philosophy.

How good was Trenton? The year before Trenton featured Andy Greene, who would go on to captain the New Jersey Devils and is still playing in the NHL. Trenton had already claimed eight state titles, and they would win six more. *USA Today* once proclaimed the Trojans the nation's best high school hockey team. In fact, Trenton's teams at all age levels had already hung so many state title banners from their rafters that when we played in their rink, I always told my players, "Don't look up." It never worked.

The *Ann Arbor News* sent a reporter to cover the action. We figured we had a chance to give Trenton a scare, until our assistant captain, Dave McMurtrie, one of our two best defensemen, caught his skate blade in a rut and fractured his fibula. *In warm-ups.*

It went downhill from there. Trenton showed us who they were, on every shift. I added to our woes by sticking with game strategies long after they had proven ineffective. The Trojans were grinding us down 6–1 through two periods when they did what championship teams do in the third, burying us with seven more goals to win 13–2.

That's right: *13–2.*

If each goal had been a touchdown, the final score would have been 91–14. If you were to count to thirteen right now, you'd get bored before you got to ten. But imagine with each number a puck ended up in your net, the other team celebrated, and their band played. By the time the game ended, we could all sing their fight song. (The previous year, a Huron captain did just that.)

When we got to the locker room, our guys were throwing their sticks and gloves around — angry, hurt, embarrassed. All that work, all that sacrifice, all that hope — for what? Was our 3-and-0 start just fool's gold?

"That's *bullshit!*" one player shouted, slamming his stick against the trash can.

"Same as last year!" another yelled.

"*Worse* than last year!" another griped. "We *never* lost 13–2!"

This was bad. As soon as I walked in I brought all of it to an immediate halt.

"*Stop!*" I said. "Sit down!"

After they'd settled in, I said, in a calm voice, "Hey, I saw what you saw. Can't sugarcoat it. We just got our asses handed to us on a silver platter."

They nodded, a little surprised I was taking this approach.

"But that doesn't matter," I added. "What matters is our principles. What's the first rule of Huron hockey?!?"

"Work hard," a few mumbled.

"What's the first rule of Huron hockey?!" I yelled.

"Work hard!" they yelled back.

We went back and forth a few more times in a call-and-response. When I was satisfied, I asked them, "Well? Did you guys work hard tonight?"

They thought about it, then concluded, yes, actually they had.

"That's right!" I said. "Everyone here *worked their asses off the entire game. Every shift. Every player! No exceptions!* Now, what's the second rule of Huron hockey?"

"Support your teammates!" they yelled, loud from the start.

"What is it?!"

"Support your teammates!!"

We went back and forth again until the walls were rocking.

"Now, did anyone here fail to do that tonight?" I asked. "Did anyone blame anyone else for not scoring enough, or letting too many goals in? Anyone?"

No, they said. Nobody had pointed fingers. Everyone had supported our goalie, and everyone else.

"That's right." I said. "You supported each other after *every single damn goal they scored!* Even *their guys* didn't do that! Now *that* is impressive! That is *hard!* But you did it! This was *heroic!*

"Now listen to me: it will never be more difficult to work hard and support your teammates the entire game than it was tonight — and *you did it!* Gentlemen, if we can do that tonight, we can do that *every* night. We keep that up, I promise you, we're going to turn this around. And let me tell you something else: *We're going to play those bastards again in two months, and it sure as hell ain't gonna be thirteen-to-two!*"

They cheered.

"I'm *proud* of you. You've already done some amazing things—but this is your greatest accomplishment. This is the most impressive."

I let that sink in. I believed it. They believed it.

"Now let's get the hell out of here and focus on our next game."

The *Ann Arbor News* reporter started his story with this: "During a locker room talk following Wednesday night's matchup against second-ranked Trenton, Huron hockey coach John Bacon couldn't have seemed prouder of his team's performance.

"'The kids played smart and they played hard,' he said. 'If they keep playing like that, we'll keep winning.'

"Strange words," the reporter wrote, "since the River Rats (3-2) were only minutes away from a 13–2 mangling at the hands of the visiting Trojans."

Those were strange words—strange to everyone but us. But we were now the ones who defined ourselves. Nobody else.

I'd love to tell you we went right out and won the next game, but that's not what happened. We lost *eight more* to complete a ten-game losing streak. Undeniably ugly on paper, but the truth was we battled hard in every one of those ten losses. I'd even go so far as to say something had changed—and for the better.

"We worked hard every night because we actually thought we could win," Beltran recalls. "We *wanted* to win. We were on board."

The source of our resilience was our two principles. We not only kept following them throughout the losing streak, but we got better at them. In my four years I can tell you with complete confidence that the ten-game losing streak was the best coaching we ever did. The players kept the wheels on, and nobody gave up.

Six weeks after our first game against Trenton, we played the Trojans again—this time at their place, with all the damn banners. The good news: goalie Steve Beltran had recovered from his broken ankle. Our other senior goalie, Allan Sheldon, had played very well all year, but I felt Beltran was his equal, and when they were both healthy, they brought out the best in each other. The bad news: Mike Henry and Elmo were out, and Dave McMurtrie was still sidelined with his fractured fibula. All things considered, for a team with little depth, this looked to be a much tougher game.

We entered the third period behind 6–0, almost exactly where we were the first time we met, before they had finished us off 13–2. Another slaughter would do some serious damage to our morale. But we played much better and tied the final period 1–1, for a 7–1 final score.

After I scanned the scoresheet in the locker room I discovered that, according to our stat keepers, we had actually outshot them 6–5 in that final period. I was sure the Trojans didn't care about that — they probably didn't even notice — but we cared a lot. I made a big deal out of it in the locker room and in my follow-up email, grabbing every positive sign I could.

Progress!

More important: we were done playing scared in front of the best team in the state — and therefore in front of anyone.

That weekend we played Kalamazoo Central, a team that had beaten Huron 5–3 the previous year. I put Beltran in again, and he notched a very satisfying 5-0 victory, to give us a 4-10 record. We had survived the worst and come out the better for it.

In the midst of the ten-game losing streak, we had lost to crosstown rival Pioneer, 5–0. Weeks before our rematch, in a brief conversation with some of the seniors I told them how, back in my day, after we scored our classmates in the stands would throw tennis balls on the ice.

"It was awesome," I said. The seniors thought so too and told some friends. Then we forgot about the subject.

In front of a packed, raucous crowd, we fell behind 3–0 but were playing so hard we never felt out of it. Near the end of the second period, Mike Henry's shot ricocheted off the glass right to Elmo, who snapped it into the net to cut the gap to 3–1.

When I looked up at the clock to see if we had enough time left to score again before the end of the period, a solid wave of fluorescent green tennis balls came flying out of the student section. Apparently the seed I'd planted with the seniors about this old ritual had taken root with their friends, one of whom went to the local tennis club to get five hundred used balls, then passed them out to his classmates that night.

"Honestly," Henry recalls, "I didn't think they were going to do it until I got hit by one. I turned around. 'What the **** are they doing?' Then I remembered, 'Ohhh, right!'"

It was awesome — and *disastrous*. The refs gave us a penalty, and our athletic director tossed out the entire student section. The wheels came off, and we lost, 7–1.

Our temporary high only made the crash that much harder. As Henry says today, "For that moment — when we were pounding Pioneer, our fans were going crazy, and the tennis balls were flying — we felt like kings! We had something Pioneer never had. Then they cleared the students out, we got beat, and the reality set in: the seniors would never get another shot at Pioneer."

The next day the story ran in full color on the front page of the *Ann Arbor News*. When I met with the AD in her office, I told her I was certain the idea had come from me, but none of us knew what the students were going to do. She said she regretted having to clear the student section, but rules are rules. Fair enough.

When I left, the AD's secretary handed me a note: "Coach, come see me in the gym. — Mike."

I went upstairs and found Mike Henry in his PE class. It felt particularly good to see him. Henry had been doing a superlative job leading the team, so when he told me, "Everyone's burnt out. You should cancel practice today," I listened.

Still, practice was sacrosanct. The players didn't skip them or show up late, we scheduled them down to the minute, and we never,

ever canceled one. But that afternoon, when I saw the guys drag themselves into the locker room, it was obvious Henry was right. Still, I knew that skipping just one practice can break hard-won habits, so I concocted a compromise.

After they sat down, I told them how proud of them I was — and now they were the coolest team in the school! They laughed at that. They'd been hearing their classmates' comments all day. The hockey team had captured the school's imagination.

Then I told them we were going to skip our prepractice workout, and I started telling some pointless stories with no message to them whatsoever, all for laughs. When I finished, I said, "The ice is available, but we're not having practice today. So you can skate if you want, but you can go home if you like too. No penalty at all."

Some went out to play some pickup hockey, others went home, but everyone came back the next day rested, relaxed, and refreshed. Henry had been right.

"I think one of the top three smartest things you ever did," Elmo recalls, "was tell us stories after the 'Tennis Ball Game' instead of practice. We were fried. It wasn't fun showing up. We were exhausted. You came into the locker room and told us funny stories about ruining your rental cars and some of your hockey memories. You sensed we were about to break, and you changed tactics. Granted, it only lasted one day, but it was enough."

The players proved it two days later by tying a top Metro League team, 2–2, in one of our best games of the year.

But of course, I wasn't the one who sensed the guys were about to break. It was Mike Henry. All I did was listen, which was easy because of the trust built between us — and that's how we spared ourselves a potential collapse.

I was always looking for some motivational hook, but what could we shoot for? Two-thirds through the schedule and we still had only one win in the Metro League and four overall. Ten wins seemed out of reach, and I didn't want to pin our hopes on the playoffs, a single-elimination format where we'd be underdogs in our first game.

Looking through a list of previous Huron hockey records one day, it came to me: the biggest improvement any Huron team had made over the previous season was five wins. We were already at plus-four with eight games left, so I told the guys we had a serious milestone to fight for: the most improved team in Huron's thirty-three-year history.

When we faced the same Metro League team we had already beaten at the start of the season, we proved it wasn't a fluke with a 5–4 win for our record-tying fifth win. With two games left, we played Dexter, a local small-town team that had tied Huron the year before with only ten players. This time we mauled them, 7–3, for our school-record sixth win.

Two days later we played another Metro League rival on Senior Night. Although Allan Sheldon had played very well to notch our last two wins, I started Beltran. He played the best game of his career to pull out a 3–2 victory, for our school-record seventh win. Leaving our home ice for the last time, Beltran, Henry, and I gave each other bear hugs — as good as it gets.

When they turned their equipment in later that week, I surprised them with a little ceremony in our locker room. We glued all ten seniors' name plaques in a line on the wall, then added another green plaque added to the left, which said:

2000–01

MOST IMPROVED TEAM (+7 WINS)

They were rightly proud of it.

At our banquet the parents presented me with a very nice watch. When I opened it, they all shouted, "5:00 means 5:00!" Even the parents were promoting our new culture.

Although Mike Henry had finished fourth on the team in scoring, his teammates — wiser than most high school kids — nonetheless voted him the team's Most Valuable Player. Why? Because they saw what I saw: Henry's value to the team wasn't his scoring but his *leadership,* and that's what we needed most. As I'd said at my first lunch with Mike, I didn't care if he didn't score a goal, so long as he led the team. He had done so, brilliantly.

Introducing the MVP award, I said, "This summer I explained to Mike Henry that we had more work to do than any team before us, so I needed help. My captain needed to be more than a good guy, which he is. He needed to be more than a good player, which he is. He needed to be more than a good captain even. What I needed was a *great* captain, one for the ages — one who had skin thick enough to risk his own popularity to say what needed to be said; one with shoulders broad enough to take on whatever task the team needed that day; and one with a heart big enough to care about everyone in our locker room. Well, we got him.

"On the questionnaire I sent out last spring, I asked what they wanted their teammates to say about them at the end of the season. Henry wrote only two words: 'Good leader.'

"Captain Henry, you were a *great* leader, the most important this program has ever seen — and at just the right time."

I told the players that, because of them, we would win more games the next year, and the year after that. By then everyone *expected* that. I concluded with this: "When we win the state title — not *if* but *when* — we will invite you back to a banquet just like this one, and I will ask you to stand, and tell the crowd what I'm going to tell you right now: that no team in Huron's long history has been more important to the program than you — and that everything the following classes will accomplish, they will accomplish on your shoulders. You are the foundation for all the success that future teams will achieve.

"Long after your playing days are done, I expect every one of you will be successful. But always remember that you were once a very special part of a very special team at a very special time — and you always will be."

I took a moment to compose myself. "I will never, ever forget you."

When it was time for the senior speeches, Mike Henry, Steve Beltran, and the other seniors pulled a tear too — proof that they were not only leading, but leading from the heart.

I couldn't ask for more.

- Make your rules few, make them clear, and connect them to your larger mission. They don't have to be *easy* to follow, but they have to be *simple.*

- Make sure your rules are within everyone's control to follow every day, because your rules are based on *behavior,* not *results.* And therefore there are no excuses.

- Focus on what your team sends out into the world, not on what comes back. That in turn allows your team to *define itself* instead of letting the world do it for them.

- Hammer your values home constantly, in every manner you can imagine, until they become *their* values, and they start instilling them in each other. When this happens, *you have changed the culture of your team.*

Building Trust

6

Let Them Surprise You

- Talent is not a constant. The biggest variable is the support you give them — or don't.

- Don't play favorites. Water all your plants equally, and watch who grows.

- You don't know the potential you're missing until you give them a chance.

L eaders too often think their people are robots: they can do what they can do, they can't do what they can't do, none of it will ever change, and there's nothing anyone can do about it.

But the truth is the opposite of all that: people *can* grow, dramatically, and that includes leaders — a lesson I learned in real time.

Once you've built a principle-based culture that sets your people on the right path, you can reap an impressive return on investment, in terms of untapped talent and effort, *just by shutting up and getting out of your people's way.*

Vital point: your employees' talents are *not* fixed — nor is their maturity or leadership ability or just about anything except their height. Further, it's impossible to predict who's going to develop and who isn't. This understanding leads to a fundamental conclusion: you work with *all of your people*, you play no favorites, and then you see who rises. Let *them* decide what they can become — and you'll be amazed by who excels, how fast, and how far. Before you know it, the unassuming worker in the middle cubicle is suddenly leading the pack — and you will have a much stronger team because of it.

We had a lot of guys who were underestimated by everyone — sometimes including me — who went on to do far more than expected at their position, or at a new position, or as a team leader. Of the fifty-four players I coached, I counted at least thirty who fit the description of "major overachiever" in some way or other — more than half. I didn't "discover" them. They discovered themselves, once they got the chance.

The list includes Bobby Chappuis, whom we moved from forward to defense his junior year. The next year the Metro League coaches named him the league's best defenseman, and he went on to play college hockey. One year behind Chappuis, Perry Merillat did the exact same thing, switching from forward to defense as a junior, then winning Metro League Defenseman of the Year as a senior. His good buddy Nick Standiford, a year younger than Perry, served on the reserve squad his freshman year, then started his sophomore year on the fourth line. But when our second line wasn't clicking, we moved Standiford up as an experiment — and the second line suddenly took off, with Nick contributing seven goals and nine assists.

The good news is, you don't need to predict who is going to excel. I hadn't predicted the success of any of those players, *but I didn't have to*. That's the point. The more the culture took hold the more I could afford to step back and get out of their way. Once everyone had internalized our principles, the coaches didn't have to worry very much about them going in the right direction. That allowed us to give the players even more opportunities to surprise us. When you get to that point, everyone is driving to contribute in unexpected ways — and now you're having fun.

What you *don't* want to do is set limits on them. Why put a ceiling on your people, or on your team? Who knows what's inside them, when it might come out, and how far they can take it?

In my first year coaching Huron, the two best players in the school, Chris "Frags" Fragner and Pete "Hairball" Heeringa, decided to stick with their AAA travel team rather than play for Huron. Given the previous team's winless record, you couldn't blame them.

I wasn't recruiting them, but our players were — and that's usually how it goes. It's the same in business: your employees recruit their friends — or they advise them not to apply. After we won seven games our first season, both Fragner and Heeringa asked to join our unofficial spring team. The duo made an immediate impact, leading our team to a 12-4 record.

Unbeknownst to me, that summer Fragner's father, who had coached Chris's little league teams, told Chris he had to choose between playing travel hockey to get a college scholarship or playing for Huron, which would mean focusing on school and forgetting his hockey dreams.

"This was the first time I faced a serious crossroads," Fragner recalls. "My mom was a teacher who always stressed education, but hockey was my life."

Honestly, I wasn't sure our program would be right for Fragner and Heeringa either. If they expected to be treated like kings and have an easy path to college hockey, Huron would not be their best choice. We didn't promise them anything other than equal treatment, but we didn't tell them Huron hockey *wasn't* for them either. True, it would take exceptional young men with different priorities than most stars to leave elite travel hockey programs to play for Huron. In fact, a few talented players in the school never came out for Huron's school team.

Anyone could see Fragner's and Heeringa's talent, but we didn't need talent alone. We needed players who wanted to buy in — and that's rare. But who was to say these two young men weren't exceptional? We explained our program and let them decide for themselves. Perhaps to everyone's surprise, including mine, Fragner and Heeringa both decided to play for Huron—but it came with a price.

"I was preparing to join a team that, two years prior, hadn't won a game all year," Fragner recalls. "The year before things started looking up [when Huron won seven games], but they still lost twice as many games as they won. [We actually lost seventeen.] Also, I would go from playing sixty games a year on the travel team to twenty-five for Huron. I was resigned to the fact that my hockey career was going to be short and less sweet than I had envisioned."

When Fragner and Heeringa, aka "Frags and Hairball," joined our summer workouts, I knew they were serious. But the painful reality was that the two talented juniors would be taking playing time from two seniors—a situation ripe for bitterness, since the seniors had all stuck with the team when it was winless, while these two had played elsewhere. So how do you bring these new guys into the fold and ensure they're accepted by the seniors?

Fragner recalls, "Coach Bacon was excited but explained that while he thought I could make an impact on the team, he would treat me the same as any other player, and no one would receive preferential treatment."

Fragner's being generous. I pulled them aside and said, "You guys are the two best players here—and that's why you won't do a single thing right in my eyes all summer." That got their attention. "You see, the seniors have been working out for a year and a half now, and they see you show up, and they probably resent it on some level. So to avoid that I'm going to be harder on you than everyone else, by far. You won't get any praise from me in front of them, I'll nitpick everything you do—and by the end of the summer, the guys will like you a lot more than they'll like me."

The two accepted the deal, they worked as hard as everyone else, and they didn't complain even once when I ragged on them for some minuscule mistake or other.

"I quickly went from thinking Huron hockey would be a casual hobby to seeing this would be no cakewalk," Fragner recalls. "For summer workouts Coach Bacon took a wide range of players and clearly laid out his expectations: 'We win and lose as a team and we dress like a team.' Everyone wore the same sweats for workouts, the same shirt and ties to games, and we respected our locker room. 'Early is on time and on time is late.' In the off-season, we'd train harder than any other team and 'fill our gas tanks' so we could out-work teams in the third period."

Frags and Hairball did all that and more. Sure enough, by the end of the summer even the seniors were taking their side against me. The plan had worked.

When the players picked captains in November, Frags earned enough votes to be an assistant — very rare for a junior — and Hair-ball was close. It didn't hurt that both players had great attitudes, put the team first, and were exemplary in just about every way. The duo also understood that our program was about more than just wins and losses, and therefore we would not be playing favorites with the stars. If they were a minute late for the bus, the bus would be gone — same as it would be for anyone else. And yet these two highly competitive players were still interested in playing for us.

"Coach Bacon took a group of mediocre players and got the most out of them," Fragner says. "He did so by communicating clearly, motivating us by doing everything right alongside us, and being our biggest supporter. Most coaches get lost in winning. They design plays for their best players and yell at the lesser players. Bacon un-derstood he had to treat everyone with the same set of rules, even himself."

Treating our two stars like everyone else reassured the rest of the team, but it also helped Frags and Hairball. Stevie Wasik explains, "If the program was all about Frags and Hairball, we never would have been able to build a culture where every single player got mea-surably better. Looking back, it's funny because, by taking emphasis off of those guys, the whole team got stronger, which in the end el-evated Frags and Hairball."

In other words, if we'd focused solely on Frags and Hairball, they wouldn't have had a strong enough team to support them. A rising tide lifts all boats.

Of course, adding players of their caliber would help us only if their character equaled their talent, or else they would have poisoned our team chemistry. I knew they had talent, but I didn't know about their character until they joined our off-season workouts.

I didn't tell them to join our team. But I didn't tell them *not* to either — and that's all they needed. Their decisions came with real consequences, but the team's culture tipped the scales. They had seen enough of the hockey world to appreciate what we were trying to accomplish.

This confirms one of my earlier points: you don't need them all, but if you build your team on strong principles, *the right ones will find you.*

Sometimes it's your team as a whole that will surprise you.

After our first winter season, we joined a summer league. Unlike during the fall league, the state allowed full-time winter coaches to work behind the bench. This was a treat for me because I could coach in shorts and sandals along with Lapper, Coach Ned, Pete Uher, and now Mike Henry, who not surprisingly proved to be a great coach.

The summer league was a notch below the Metro League, but stronger than our previous fall league. I privately hoped to win half of our ten games, though I never told them that. The main thing was to get everyone equal playing time and lots of experience.

But a funny thing happened: we looked up with two games left to see we were tied for first place with a 6-1-1 record. In our penultimate game, however, we fell behind 4–1 after two periods, all but knocking us out of the running. Worse, we would have to start the third period a man down, killing a penalty. On paper, we were cooked.

I knew we were good enough to beat that team, but a three-goal deficit is a hell of a thing to overcome. In the locker room before the third period, nobody felt like a "chalk-talk" or a "win one for the Gipper" speech — including me.

I decided we weren't going to get there with rational analysis or a lot of yelling. No, it was time for some magical thinking. With a breezy manner, I walked to the middle of the room, spun my clipboard casually in the air, and let it hit the floor. After it made a satisfying *smack!*, their heads snapped. I grinned and said, "So, who wants to be part of the greatest comeback in the history of Huron hockey?"

I had no way of knowing if that was true. In more than eight hundred Huron hockey games, a few teams must have pulled off bigger comebacks — and this was only an unofficial summer league game anyway. But who cared? You wanna dream? Make it a good one!

They looked pleasantly surprised to see I was in no mood for ranting and raving. They responded enthusiastically, popping out of their mental rut.

"Good!" I said. "Here's how we're going to do it! When we start the period killing a penalty, Yooper is going to sweep their puck carrier over to Moran, who is going to crush him, and the puck is going to pop loose right to Frags, who's going to go down and score. Then it's 4–2, we have plenty of time, and we're going to pound them until we score three more goals. And that's going to be it. Now, who's with me?"

"Yeah!"

"Let's do it!"

"Great!" I said. "Now let's go have some fun — at their expense!"

What happened next still amazes me. Starting the period one man down, we dumped the puck into their zone, Yooper swept their puck carrier over to Moran, who crushed him. The puck popped loose right to Fragner, who went down and scored — *exactly what I had told them would happen.*

Everyone went nuts. A few of the guys on the bench turned

around and looked at me wide-eyed, like I was Nostradamus. Staying in character, the happy-go-lucky coach of a team predestined to pull off a miracle, I just shrugged, palms up, and asked, "Did you ever doubt me?" But the truth was this: I didn't doubt *them*. My faith in their potential allowed me to claim we were about to pull off a historic upset.

Just like that, it was 4–2. We were a new team, controlling play, but with 1:40 left, we were still down two goals. Before a face-off, I told our goalie to come to the bench at the 1:00 mark so we could replace him with an extra attacker. But then the dam finally broke, and we scored on a rebound, leaving us down just 4–3.

Eight seconds later, our third line scored to tie the game, 4–4.

Sixteen seconds after that we scored again to give us a 5–4 lead. *Three goals in twenty-four seconds.*

With a minute left, *their* coaches had to call a time-out, not us, so they could pull *their* goalie. When our goalie came back to our bench during the time-out, we laughed. I told him our plans had changed, and maybe we shouldn't pull him with a one-goal lead. Twenty-four seconds later, Fragner zipped the puck from half-ice into their open net.

Final score: 6–4. With one game left, the summer league title was ours to lose.

"It was one of those moments you start to believe in yourself," Elmo recalls. "Our first year we found ways to lose. Now we were finding ways to win."

In the locker room our guys were whooping and hollering, happily stunned by what they'd done. "We were losing our marbles," Elmo says.

In our next game, the last of our summer league, we played a team that had beaten us three times in the previous nine months, including our only loss that summer. But our guys were on a mission and won, 4–3, to claim a nice big trophy. True, it was just a summer league title, it wasn't official, and it didn't really count for much. But so what? It was the first trophy of any kind Huron had earned in years, a nice reward for all their hard work, and it meant everything to them.

How'd we do it? The coaches got out of the players' way, so they could surprise us. In short, we let them lead.

Three months later, at our winter team tryouts in November, we had an embarrassment of riches. Our numbers had doubled from thirty-five guys trying out our first year to seventy, including an influx of skilled newcomers: freshmen who were ready to play varsity, talented transfers from other schools, plus Frags and Hairball.

That was great news, but we already had ten seniors returning, and eight juniors. If we were a win-at-all-cost program, we would have cut a few seniors to make room for younger players with potential, but the coaches rightly never considered cutting any of the guys who had helped turn the program around.

But that meant we had a lot of tough decisions to make. After our next-to-last tryout day, I asked to meet with two sophomores who had played their freshman year on our "taxi squad"—a status unique to hockey teams, I believe. "Taxi players" practice with the team but don't play in the games. This helps younger players improve without taking an older player's spot on the roster. During games the taxi players fill water bottles, carry pucks, and take statistics, then play on varsity the next year.

I pulled the two players, Stevie Wasik and Bobby Shahidehpour, out into a quiet hallway. "Look, you're both ready to play varsity, but with a logjam of players in front of you, we need you to put in another year on the taxi squad."

If I didn't like telling them that, they liked hearing it even less.

"Coach, I *really* want to play on the varsity," Wasik said. "Whatever it takes."

"Me too," Shahidehpour said. They were respectful, but dead serious.

"But we're already going to have twenty-two skaters on varsity," I explained, "and we can only dress eighteen skaters for each game." As it was, barring injuries, I'd have to pick four players per game to sit out — a painful biweekly exercise. "You two would make six."

"We don't have to dress for every game," Wasik countered.

"Stevie," I said, "if I put you on varsity, you probably wouldn't dress for *half* the games. I've already got ten seniors, and eight juniors. They'll come first."

"I don't care," Wasik said, tears welling. "Coach, *I would rather fill water bottles for Huron than be captain of my travel team.*"

This got me, but I had to follow up. "Will you complain?" I asked.

"No, Coach," they said in unison, earnestly shaking their heads.

"You won't forget this conversation?"

"No, Coach!" they said, and Wasik added, "We just want to be on varsity."

They had both worked their tails off for more than a year, doing all the grunt work expected of taxi players and playing very well on our off-season teams. They expected their patience and good work to be rewarded. They had a good argument.

"Let me talk to the assistants and get back to you," I said. "No promises."

"We know. Thanks, Coach!"

After bouncing it off the staff, we decided that if they wanted it that badly, and if they kept their word about not complaining, we couldn't deny that kind of commitment. After our final tryout day, Wasik and Shahidehpour crowded around the list on the wall and saw their names under "VARSITY." They were ecstatic.

Wasik still remembers driving home and crossing a road named, yes, "Varsity."

"As soon as I saw the big white letters on the bright green street sign — VARSITY — I immediately burst into tears. *Varsity.* I'd made it."

The players were now selling the program to themselves. Making varsity, even with limited game time, was worth celebrating.

Wasik got in only nine of twenty-seven games that year, and

Shahidehpour just seven, by far the fewest on the team. But most impressively, they kept their word. They did everything we asked, never complained when they weren't in the lineup, and played their hearts out when they got their chance. They both managed to score goals, which thrilled them, and they were poised to make bigger contributions the next two years.

I'll say it again: don't tell people what they can't do — and give me the grinders who will fill water bottles just to be on the team any day.

Wasik, by the way, would be named captain his senior year, as a second-line center. He went on to work for Insight Global, an IT staffing firm based in Atlanta. His CEO, Bert Bean, talks about "feeding the hungry": help those who want your help. No need to force-feed anyone. If you're not hungry for what we're serving, that's fine. Keep walking. But if you are, keep eating. We'll get you more.

Well, Wasik wasn't the rookie of the year on our team, or at Insight Global, but he was hungry. In both cases it took him longer than his peers to get going, but once he started rolling, there was no stopping him. During Wasik's rise at Insight Global, I was invited to speak at the company's national conferences three times, and each time I couldn't resist mentioning the kid with tears in his eyes begging to fill water bottles to be on varsity.

That kid just became a vice president at age thirty-three. He started Insight Global's new Compass Division, which teaches leadership and culture to the company's corporate clients, and he hired his former coach to work on some projects with him.

And if Wasik asks me to fill water bottles, I'll do it, and do it with enthusiasm.

Matt Rolen was a good-looking, stylish kid, a big man on campus with or without hockey. But he had not played the year before I took over, and he hadn't come to our off-season workouts either. At our first tryouts, however, we took him anyway, mainly on potential.

His attitude and effort that year were okay, but only okay. So when he missed the senior banquet to visit his father in Florida without telling us, I let it go, figuring I'd never see him again. I believed we were offering something special, but if Rolen didn't think so — well, we weren't for everyone.

To my surprise, two weeks later Rolen called, asking to play for our spring team.

"I didn't see you at the banquet," I said.

"I should've told you. My mistake." I let the silence grow. "No excuse, sir."

Good enough, I decided. Now it was up to him.

Rolen became a model citizen. When we moved him from forward to defense, he threw himself into his new position, and it worked. That summer Rolen impressed me even more by becoming a *leader*. When we started our regular season in November, Rolen's teammates voted him an assistant captain.

Early that season Rolen scored two goals, briefly earning a spot on the Metro League's leaderboard. I pointed to the stats on our locker-room wall and said, "Not bad for a guy who was a fourth-line forward a year ago."

"Yeah," he said, with a grin. "And that's two more goals than you ever scored!"

"Why you little —!"

Well, he'd earned it.

Nate Reichwage's story was even more unlikely.

My first year coaching the Rats, Nate was a sophomore goalie, a shy, unassuming character everyone liked. He showed up for every workout that off-season, but during my first tryouts he couldn't stop a beach ball. We already had four goalies ahead of him, one or two more than teams normally take, but Nate had a few factors going for him: our two best goalies were both seniors; one of them, Beltran, had broken his ankle right before tryouts; and finally, I just

didn't have the heart to cut Nate. So we decided to have the freshman goalie and Nate split the fourth goalie spot by alternating practices.

"I was clearly the least skilled goaltender on the team," Nate recalls. "The most important thing that Coach Bacon taught me was
work ethic. I remember working so hard during practice and getting so angry when I let in goals."

Nate might have ranked last in talent, but no one appreciated
being on the team more.

"My fondest high school memories revolve around one thing:
Huron hockey," he says. "Sitting in those tiny desks at school, all
I could think about was seeing my teammates and coaches at the
rink. I felt part of something."

Nate worked his tail off, but by the middle of our second season, Nate's junior year, he was still stuck at third string. Our top
two goalies had played great on our off-season teams, but they had
started squabbling with each other, which affected their play. During the first half of the season, we were outshooting teams two-to-
one but had only a 6-5 record to show for it, which was driving everyone crazy. But no one dared say a peep about our goaltending
issues for fear of rattling our goalies' already fragile confidence.

Right before winter break we had one more Metro League game,
against seventh-ranked Grosse Pointe South – a highly disciplined
team that had beaten Huron 5-0, 7-2, and 7-0 in our last three
meetings. In fact, Huron had *never* beaten GPS. To add a little more
pressure, the *Ann Arbor News* would be covering the game.

After practice the day before the game, I took five assistant
coaches to a steakhouse for a free meal, something every unpaid assistant could use. When I asked them which goalie they would start,
two said the junior, two said the sophomore, and one said, "Just pull
the goalie and play with an open net all night." (It would have been
funnier if he was kidding.) No one picked Nate.

Nonetheless, I was considering starting Nate, if for no other reason than to give him a chance and send a message. I called Coach
Ned, who often worked with the goalies.

"If I start Nate tonight, can you give him all the coaching and confidence you can?"

"Absolutely!" Coach Ned loved the idea. That helped.

Because I wanted to avoid Nate freaking out, I didn't tell him he'd be starting until he got to the rink on game night. When the players arrived, I pointed to the board and said, "Nate's starting, and I know you've all got his back."

But I have to confess two things: First, although I think leaders should almost never chew out their people in public, I was so sick of the goalie drama that I had written a two-page speech to deliver after our inevitable butt-kicking, taking the two starting goalies to task for their selfish feud, which was impacting the whole team.

Second, before everyone got dressed, I called the defensemen into the coaches' room and told them they needed to play as if we had pulled the goalie, leaving an open net: take every shooter, and block every shot they could. Then I called our twelve forwards into the coaches' room — an even tighter squeeze — and gave them the same instructions. They understood.

Coach Ned, God bless him, reinforced some fundamentals with Nate and pumped him with all the confidence he could. Before the face-off Ned set up shop right behind Nate's net with a notebook, so Nate could see Coach Ned give him the thumbs-up after every stop in play.

Despite all our precautions, when the puck dropped, I still expected the worst. Heck, I almost welcomed a blowout to set up my postgame screed. I just wanted to get the massacre over with, rip our two starting goalies, and start over after the break.

But when Grosse Pointe South's starting center fired the game's first shot, Nate Reichwage made the save, then swept the puck into the corner, just like you're supposed to. After the first whistle, Nate looked behind him and saw Coach Ned giving him two thumbs-up.

Well, one-for-one. Our defensemen smothered the Blue Devils' second shot, and our forwards blocked their third. They were taking their mission seriously — and it didn't hurt that they all liked

Nate and wanted to see him survive the night intact. Then Nate made three more saves and started looking like he'd been doing it his whole life.

"I was extremely nervous and excited at the same time," Nate recalls. "I obsessively went through my movements in the crease to make sure I was centered in the net and cutting down the angles."

Inspired, our guys mounted an unlikely 2–0 first-period lead. But I knew the real test would occur after Nate let in a goal, especially if it was a bad one. Once the dam breaks, anything can happen. But after GPS scored late in the first period — on a good shot — Nate's teammates swarmed him in support, Coach Ned stood up and pointed to his head and heart, and Nate kept his head screwed on straight.

With five minutes left in the game, we were down just 3–2, about ten goals closer than I expected to be. I couldn't believe we actually had a chance to beat such a good team, but there we were. With Nate playing well enough to free our forwards, we scored two more goals plus an open-netter to seal a shocking 5–3 upset.

"Coach Bacon gave me a chance," Nate remembers, "and I tried to make the most of that opportunity."

The guys were thrilled for the team and for Nate, mobbing him in front of his net and whooping it up all the way to our locker room. In the *Ann Arbor News,* the Grosse Pointe South coach was gracious: "I see a very disciplined team out there. He's got them believing in the system he wants to play."

Of course, he gave me far too much credit, not knowing I had gone into the game fully prepared to get blown out by his top-end team yet again. None of it would have worked if it wasn't for the quiet kid who finally got his chance. Our guys had held a superb team to just twenty-three shots, and Nate Reichwage had stopped twenty of them, for an 87 percent success rate — the best we'd seen from any of our goalies since we'd won our summer league.

When I walked into our raucous locker room, I ducked into the coaches' office to pull out my two-page rant about the other goalies, tear it up, and throw it in the trash. No need for that now. Then I high-fived the assistants and gave Coach Ned a bear hug.

To this day, I cannot tell you for the life of me what the hell happened that night. The same goalie who had ranked last for a year and a half had just stonewalled one of the best teams in the state — and it wasn't because we'd given him some great secret, or a vision came to him in a dream, or a genie had shown up with three wishes. No doubt Nate's attention to detail in practice had produced incremental improvements that I had probably missed due to my obsession with our other goalies. Perhaps Nate was also a gamer who saved his best performance for the big stage. I honestly don't know.

But I do know that the goalie I saw that night was not to be dismissed. I believed Nate's debut was for real, and we made him the starter. He removed any doubts when he went on to win nine games against just four losses and two ties. What he had shown us that first night turned out to be who he really was.

"Nate was super-untested, super-quiet, just kind of there," Elmo recalls. "Then he absolutely goes Hulk mode [in his first game] and gives us confidence in our goaltender for the first time all year."

When you set up a strict meritocracy where everyone gets an honest chance, it motivates *everyone*. Starters have to work to keep their jobs, and backups are motivated to take those jobs. People want to play on a team that's fair, which inspires them to do their best.

The other two goalies not only accepted Nate being made the starter — liking Nate might have been the only thing they had in common — they seemed relieved to end their feud. Nate kept the top spot for the rest of his high school career, earning a nice feature story in the *Ann Arbor News*, the nickname Darth Nater from his teammates, and the team's Most Improved Player award.

We did just one thing for Nate Reichwage, which turned out to be all he needed: we never told him what he couldn't do.

Like Nate Reichwage, your people can and will do amazing things too, if you just give them a chance and get out of their way.

- Talent is not fixed, nor is maturity, grit, or leadership ability. If you give them opportunities and support, anyone can grow.

- Don't try to predict who's going to succeed and who isn't. Get out of the prediction business. Get into the production and promotion business.

- Treat everyone fairly, *including the quiet ones.* Some shoot right up, and others will lie dormant for years before sprouting. You need only to sit back and let them surprise you.

7

You Can't Motivate People You Don't Know

- There is nothing more important for any leader than getting to know your people.
- If you want your people to trust you, you have to trust them first.
- When you trust each other, you can make difficult decisions with confidence.

From Knute Rockne's "win one for the Gipper" to Herb Brooks's "this moment is yours," we're suckers for a great locker-room speech — a uniquely American oral tradition. Americans are so fascinated with locker-room lectures that major companies will pay $100,000 just to hear famous coaches tell their tales for an hour.

I'm guiltier of this obsession than most, having written many stories about those speeches and given plenty of talks myself. When I coached, I took very seriously every chance I had to talk to my guys, and I like to think those speeches helped. These days I give dozens of speeches every year to companies and organizations across North America, and obviously I like to think those are worthwhile too.

But if delivering a paint-peeling pep talk isn't your thing, I have good news: it might be the most overrated device in a leader's toolbox.

I have encountered many great leaders who were, at best, mediocre speakers — and that might be charitable. John Wooden rarely even bothered to give a pregame speech, and Bowling Green's Hall of Fame football coach Doyt Perry's pregame speeches were so comically ineffective that he felt compelled to delegate that duty to his assistants. The typical pregame speech from my mentor at Culver Academies, Al Clark, consisted of nine words, delivered in a soft monotone: "Well, this would be a good game to win."

Thanks, Coach!

Didn't matter. Al Clark won 1,017 games, more than any high school hockey coach in history — and it wasn't because of his locker-room pep talks.

My suspicion that motivational speeches aren't as important as we think was confirmed after I designed and taught a new course at the University of Michigan I called "Leading by Coaching." We studied dozens of great coaches — from John Wooden to Pat Summit, Eddie Robinson, and Michigan's NCAA-champion softball coach Carol Hutchins — through readings, videos, and guest lectures, and compared them to the worst coaches my students had played for. Then we teased out the elements that made each coach stand out, for better or worse, and organized those traits into three categories: essential, negotiable, and deal-breakers.

I was not surprised when my students decided that dishonesty, distrust, and bullying were all deal-breakers. But my eyebrows rose when they quickly concluded that motivational speaking was "negotiable." Some of the coaches we studied were truly spellbinding speakers — Green Bay's Vince Lombardi and "Miracle on Ice" coach Herb Brooks top that list — while others rarely even tried to give pregame speeches. Did it matter? I know Lombardi's and Brooks's players would tell you it did, just as surely as Wooden's and Clark's players would tell you it didn't.

But why? I now believe that what happens *before* a great locker-room speech is more important than the speech itself. The elements that lead up to great speeches – knowing your players' backgrounds, getting your work done in the preseason, and having your finger on the team's pulse to that point – prime the players for the final spark of inspiration when the coach walks in before the game. What came before is the steak. The speech is merely the sizzle.

The best speeches are usually not spontaneously pulled from thin air, either, but patiently prepared like a bonfire – slowly constructed and soaked in fuel until the moment comes to light the match, toss it on the wood, and set the room on fire. If all those elements aren't present prior to the speech, the speech won't work. But if those elements are plentiful, even Al Clark saying, "Well, this would be a good game to win," is enough.

Okay, if "win one for the Gipper" speeches aren't essential, what is?

The answer that came most often from our research, our guest lectures, and my students again and again was this: great leaders always know their people. *Always*. And that's why the best leaders make that their top priority.

Why is this of such paramount importance? One of my mentors, Huron's former assistant principal Al Gallup, a World War II veteran who's still biking every day at ninety-four, told me years ago, "It's hard to motivate people you don't know."

I put that one in my pocket, and I've repeated it many times since.

Your résumé, your title, your tactics, your fancy speeches – none of it counts for much if your employees don't already know you care about them as people. Stumble over that first hurdle and you won't be clearing many after that.

So how do you do it?

Here's the scary part: if you want to know your people, you have to let them know you – and you have to go first.

In most journalism classes they advise interviewers to avoid talking about themselves and to keep the focus on the subject. True enough to a point, or you won't get many quotes. But I've found the opposite to be just as important: if you don't share some of yourself first and trust the interviewee with it, then why should they trust you?

Before I went around Captain Henry's back deck to meet the players I'd just inherited, I knew I had to go first. The more you share, the more they're going to share. That's how you begin to develop trust with your people. Then I asked a bit about each player, starting with their names. That too was essential. From our first day, I never once had to call anyone, "Hey, you!"

How do you get to know your people better? All the usual ways —plus a hundred more. We learned about each other during our workouts, practices, study tables, team dinners, bus trips, and just hanging out in the locker room. We also bonded early each season by doing a ropes course, playing paintball, and traveling to Thanksgiving tournaments. None of these experiences by themselves meant much. But taken together, they meant everything.

In those days a lot of players would talk with me on AOL's Instant Messenger (AIM). These days they text. One way or the other, I talked with them constantly, probably interacting with every player at least a little bit every day.

I liked to talk with the players on our bus rides, catching up row by row during our forty-minute trips "downriver." On the way back from Trenton one night the bus driver, a woman named Nola, said to me, "You care a lot about these guys."

Her comment surprised me. "Yes, I do. But how did you know?"

She shrugged. "You can just tell."

I also visited the school at least once a week to handle this or that and usually ended up spending an hour or two just walking through the halls, the cafeteria, and the gym, running into our guys in their natural environment. The business concept of "management by walking around" is *essential* to your success. Now you can also do it by email, text, and Zoom — provided you're just checking in, with no agenda.

Most of our players played another sport, something we strongly encouraged. I saw all the guys play their other sports at least once each season. By roaming the athletic fields, I could watch a third-string defenseman dominate in tennis, or see one of our star hockey players come off the bench in a baseball game to pinch-hit. Each time you see them you learn more about them — and hopefully they see that you care.

Even better, the more the players got to know me, the less they feared approaching me. If they wanted to talk after practice or a game in the coaches' room, the answer was always yes — *always*. Didn't matter who it was or what it was about. I extended this policy to instant messages, calls, or meetups at a local restaurant at 10 p.m., when I was exhausted, because one of the players had to get something off his chest.

The answer is always yes.

What struck me about those casual conversations was how often things I really needed to know would pop up. By keeping the conversation going, you learn things you'd never hear otherwise.

When I asked for their memories while writing this book, I was surprised by how few could remember our games, and how many recalled just shooting the breeze in the locker room, at team dinners, or on the bus.

Bobby Chappuis, one of our star defensemen, says some of his best memories go back to when "Bacon would ask some of his players for an informal chat in the coaches' room. We'd talk about anything that was going on at the time, not limited to on-ice. Those moments never felt forced, but they gave us two things: One, our staff cared about the team, the players, and showed their support of us by spending extra time just to hear what was going on in our world. And two, these sessions broke down the barrier between coach and player, giving the staff more unfiltered understanding of the challenges that we were facing at the moment. If you were upset by your position in the lineup last week, you could mention that to the staff and see what you needed to do to raise your position. Or if you were struggling in a class and had a test coming, you'd talk about that."

I don't buy for a second the notion of "quality time." There's only *time*, and wherever you spend it, that's what you care about — and everyone knows it. You can't fool your people. Henry David Thoreau said the price of anything is the amount of life you exchange for it. Whatever else we coaches got right or wrong, the players knew that all of us were exchanging a lot of our lives to work with them — and we were happy to make the trade.

But — and I need to be crystal-clear about this — we didn't spend that time with our players because we felt obligated to, or because we wanted to get inside information or gain a competitive edge. No, we just liked them, and we liked being around them. Like I said, the assistant coaches joined the team at first as a favor to me, but they stayed because it was fun for them to spend time with people they trusted, respected, and enjoyed.

Here's something familiar to every parent: your kids don't have to love you, but you have to love them. When your kid yells, "I hate you!" you can't yell back, "Yeah, well, I hate you too!"

Not an option.

"If you don't like someone in your office," our former captain Stevie Wasik observes, "the sad truth is, they already know."

When that happens, take some advice from Abe Lincoln, who once said, "I don't like that man. I must get to know him better." It usually works.

We all worked to make the locker room a safe place for everyone, but Mike Henry's senior class took it a step further, talking to the freshmen at school, driving them to practice across town, and even occasionally taking them to lunch.

One of our first team's freshmen, Chris Kwon, who had started playing hockey just two years earlier, recalls the time Henry and some seniors pulled him out of the cafeteria to take him to the nearest Wendy's. "I walked out of the cafeteria door amongst guys at the time I felt were a foot taller than me and I felt like a boss," Kwon remembers. "Those guys always lifted my spirits and made me feel part of the team. I can't thank that senior class enough. They raised my standards of who I wanted to become." Kwon became All-State.

Early on I invited a good friend, Dale Rominski, who'd won two NCAA titles for Michigan and played in the NHL before concussions cut his career short, to work with our team in his new role as a sports psychologist. His Friday visits with the players quickly became a high point for them.

"I remember after my first visit with the team saying to myself, 'Wow, they really paid attention,'" he says today. "It was clear the kids were invested. It was also clear that [the] players felt safe. There was self-esteem, an absence of anxiety. Safety and security was reinforced by the team rules. Their shared experience created belonging."

When we took over the program, that's what I wanted to build.

You want to get to know your people better? It's simple — but not easy. There are no shortcuts. You have to see them in a dozen different places and have a hundred conversations. Do that and you'll enjoy them more, they might even start to like you, and when you need something from them, they'll be much more likely to come through.

When I saw one of my guys walking down the school hallway, I didn't have to yell, tell him to turn around, or correct his behavior. I needed only to say his name, in a voice they'd already heard a thousand times, and they'd respond immediately. That wasn't discipline. That was mutual respect — built on countless conversations.

The better you know your people, the better you can make decisions about them, including the tough calls. Knowing your people also helps you sense when to give them a break. If one of our players came to me sincerely with a problem, we could discuss a lot of things. If I felt they were trying to pull one over (which almost never happened), all bets were off. But when in doubt, I'd rather look like a fool than a jerk — and sometimes those are your only options.

On our team, if you missed one of our two practices before our next game, you didn't get to play in that game. That solved a lot of problems and squashed a lot of excuses. But one time it created a conundrum when the mother of our star sophomore defenseman, Jeff Marley, called an hour before a Thursday practice to let me know that Jeff was suffering one of his debilitating migraine headaches. Because Jeff had told his mom about our rule, however, she made it clear to me that if he needed to practice to play that Saturday, she'd bring him down and he would gut it out.

Well, what could have been a dicey call was made a lot easier because I knew Jeff Marley, and so did his teammates. On a team of hard workers, we all regarded Marley as one of the hardest workers. He loved being part of the team and battling with his buddies, and he was the last guy to make an excuse.

I didn't have to question if Jeff really had a migraine, or if he would suffer through a practice to play that weekend if I insisted on it. And for all those reasons, I was willing to consider putting aside our ironclad rule.

I met with our captains, laid out the situation, and asked for their opinions.

"No one works harder than Jeff," one captain said.

"Marley's not bullshitting," a senior defenseman said. "He never does."

"But," I said, playing devil's advocate, "I'd have to make an exception and explain it to the team."

"Yeah," another said. "That's your call. But they'll understand."

I agreed, strongly, but it was good to get their input. I had to tell the rest of the team — and not right before we got dressed for our game Saturday night, but as soon as they had all arrived for practice that day. I went over everything, including our rules, Mrs. Marley's call, and the fact that I'd talked to the seniors (without divulging their comments — this was on me, not them). Then I explained my decision.

"As you guys know," I said, "I don't like to make exceptions, and I've never made one for this rule. But you guys also know Jeff Marley. You know he'd come to practice if I asked him, which is why I'm making an exception: Jeff will stay home and get better today, return to practice tomorrow, and play on Saturday. But I want to be clear: this decision has nothing to do with Jeff's ability, but his character. If he wasn't a starter, I'd make the exact same call, for the exact same reasons."

His teammates didn't give an ounce of pushback, just a lot of nods. I got the very strong feeling that if I'd made Jeff come down that day to practice, his teammates would have resented me for it — and for good reason. Jeff's migraine subsided by the next day, he practiced Friday, he played on Saturday, and no one complained.

We faced a trickier situation with another player, whom I'll call Tyler Garrison (not his real name). Everyone liked Tyler, who always worked hard and supported his teammates, whether he was in the lineup or not.

So I was very disappointed to find out his junior year that he'd been arrested for "minor in possession of alcohol" with a couple of friends who were not on the team. After discussing it with Jane Bennett, the athletic director, we decided not to kick Tyler off the team. We felt that would have only made the situation worse. If he lost the structure and discipline of the team, he would probably only drink more. So I doubled the school's suspension to four games — one-sixth of our season — and put him on a urine testing program to make sure he stayed clean.

Tyler got the message, and all was well for a couple of months until one morning I got a call from the athletic director.

"It's about Tyler."

My heart sank.

"The results of his latest test came back positive. He doesn't know this yet."

We considered our options, including dismissing him from the team.

"But," she said, "we do get false positives occasionally. Could be cold medicine in his system. When you tell him the results, if he's guilty, he'll be ready for the news and he'll have some excuses ready. If he's innocent, he'll respond immediately, upset and maybe defiant, defending himself to the hilt that he was clean and the test is wrong."

I didn't know how Tyler was going to respond, or what I would do about it, though kicking him off the team was surely the simplest option. My boss gave me one more thing to think about.

"You know Kent Overbey," she asked, referring to the school's humanities history teacher and renowned track coach. "He always says, 'When in doubt, bet on the kid.'"

That stayed with me. A few hours later at the rink, while the guys were gathering in the locker room for practice, I called Tyler into the coaches' office.

"What is it, Coach?" He was upbeat and chipper, not sensing any trouble coming.

"Tyler, I've got some bad news. Jane Bennett, the athletic director, called to tell me you failed your latest urine test."

He instantly got his back up. "No way, Coach! I've been clean — I swear! I don't know how that could have happened."

"So you're telling me you haven't been drinking since you got busted?"

"That's right! None! Ask the guys!"

As silly as that might sound, I figured they'd probably know. I looked at Tyler square in the eye and waited a few beats before responding.

"All right. You've declared yourself. I'll need to talk to the AD. I want you to know it'd break my heart to lose you, but I can't make any promises."

Tyler left, visibly shaken, a state reflected in his play during practice. Afterward I asked the captains, discreetly, if they thought Tyler might be drinking again.

"I think he's been taking it seriously," one said. The others agreed.

Well, here we go. I felt it wouldn't be fair to the team or to Tyler to let this linger. I had to make a decision by the next day. After more talks with the assistant coaches and the athletic director, I still wasn't sure what to do. If I let Tyler back on the team, I was sticking my neck out pretty far. What if he was duping me? What if he got caught again?

But something in Tyler's response got to me. I also knew if I kicked Tyler off the team, nothing we cared about was likely to get better: his conduct, his grades, his buddies, his future. I decided to take Kent Overbey's advice and bet on the kid.

When Tyler arrived early for practice the next day, my door was open.

"Coach?" He asked nervously.

"C'mon in here, Tyler. Close the door. Sit down. I've talked to a lot of guys and I've given this a lot of thought. I don't know what happened with the test, but I've known you for a few years now, and I've decided to bet on you."

He looked relieved and grateful — even a little emotional.

"Now look," I said, "if you fail another test, nothing else will matter. You'll be gone from the team no matter what you or I say or do. We'll keep in touch. I won't give up on you — but you'll be gone from the program. Understood?"

"I know, Coach — I know. Thanks, Coach. I won't let you down."

I nodded. "I'm betting you won't. But I'll have to explain this to the team."

He bowed. This was the medicine he had to take.

When our workout was supposed to start, I told the guys to sit down. Then I laid out the situation. I quoted Kent Overbey's line and told them, "So that's what I'm doing here: I'm betting on Tyler. He will need your support, and I know you'll give it to him. I'm doing this because I know Tyler, he's got a lot of credit with me, and I think with you too, and I'm confident he'll come through."

I saw a lot of players agreeing with that.

"And if he doesn't," I concluded, looking to add a little levity, "I'll kill him with my bare hands."

For the rest of that season and the next, Tyler was a model citizen. He rose to third-line winger and became a good penalty killer. Not an All-Stater, but a solid contributor. Mainly, though, we just liked having Tyler on the team. He was a good guy who worked hard, supported his teammates, and was fun to be around. He was one of us.

Tyler went to college, started a good career, and always — *always* — comes back for our annual team barbecue.

Kent Overbey was right: when in doubt, bet on the person. But you can only do that if you really *know* the person. If I hadn't known Tyler, I wouldn't have fought for him, he would have lost a good opportunity, we would have lost a good teammate, and I would have lost a good friend.

- **Leadership depends far less on rousing speeches than on getting to know your people.**
- **There is no such thing as quality time. There's just time, and how you spend it is what you care about. If you spend it on your people, they know they matter to you.**
- **If you want your people to trust you, you first have to trust them, and open yourself up.**
- **When you know your people well, you can make decisions you'd never dare make otherwise. You can bet on them when others won't. If you can make difficult calls with conviction, your people will notice, and they will gain confidence in you.**

8

———

I Work Hard for You,
You Work Hard for Me

- You have to work harder than your people do — and they need to see that.

- If you're working hard, it's fair for you to expect them to work hard. That's the deal.

- There is no reason to be stingy with praise — especially for those who need it most.

You already know we asked a lot of our players — probably more than any coaches in the state were asking. So why didn't any of our guys quit?

First, because they proved to be much tougher, stronger, and more dedicated than anyone had given them credit for — including me. Just about everyone had told me the exact opposite about them. Fact is, no one knew what these guys had inside them because no one had ever tested them to find out.

Second, because we always tried to give them more in return. I came up with a lot of slogans, but I was always interested to see which ones meant the most to them. Those became *our* mantras. This one they repeated often: "I work hard for you. You work hard for me."

Once the players established that they were willing to work hard and support their teammates, there wasn't much I wasn't willing to do for them. Simple example: if they wanted something to help them be more competitive, we found a way to get it for them.

You want to take a fancy charter bus to our overnight Thanksgiving tournament? We'll set up a car wash to raise $2,000 and reserve the bus.

You guys want nice North Face black fleece sweats, with the Huron "H" and your number stitched in gold? We'll get them for you.

You want your classmates to know what you're accomplishing? I'll be sure to send the school a brief announcement after every game to put out on the school PA system, and I'll work my journalism contacts to pitch stories on you guys to the *Ann Arbor News,* the Detroit papers, and TV and radio stations. Our guys probably got as much publicity as any high school team—but they deserved it. They were a hell of a story!

Our first year together we weren't able to get any of our guys on the All-Metro League squads, let alone All-State. But from our second season on, we worked hard to make sure everyone got the attention they deserved. I sent out releases to the two hundred or so coaches around the state who voted on these things. It's impossible to say if it helped, but over three years, twenty-seven of our players made one of the All-Metro League teams; four were named the Metro League's best forward or defenseman; nineteen made Academic All-State, ten All-State Honorable Mention, seven first-team All-State; and Chris Fragner earned Mr. Hockey runner-up. Our players got as much recognition as anyone.

I battled refs on their behalf too. I could be tough on our players, but once we walked out of our locker room, it was "us against the world." So once, when a game was getting out of hand and one of our opponents shoved our player into the boards headfirst, seconds

after he'd scored a goal, I told the ref the game had become danger-
ous — and he kicked me out. It was embarrassing, but as I walked
from our bench to the lobby, our parents stood and cheered. An opponent's mom asked if they were cheering because they didn't like
the head coach. No, Beltran's mom said, "we're cheering *for* the head
coach, because he's defending our sons."

Need help writing a paper? At our Monday night study tables,
which we created to make sure everyone stayed on top of their
schoolwork, I put aside my own work and helped them out with
theirs — or the next night after practice, or the next.

Even the demands we made on them seemed to have a positive
effect. Our high standards didn't make it harder to get good people
to try out. They made it *easier,* and high standards will do the same
for you. Harvard, West Point, and Teach for America, hell, they
don't apologize for their high standards. They *brag* about them, because that's the point — the reason why people want to take on those
daunting challenges. On our team we sold the hard, and the players bought it, because they sensed a deep compliment embedded in
those expectations: they could do this. And soon they were selling
it to others.

"Some of the little things have stuck with me longer than the
games and the goals," said Bobby Chappuis, grandson of Heisman
Trophy runner-up Bob Chappuis. "One of those was the [Monday
night] study hall. What stood out was the expectation that you were
there ten minutes early and that you were diligently studying for the
entire two hours. You sat a certain way in your seat and did not talk.
Coach Bacon took these sessions seriously. I can't say study table
was fun, but it felt good to be with a group of teammates that believed we were doing something that mattered."

We weren't just selling the hard, but also celebrating the sense
of purpose, accountability, and belonging that goes with high expectations.

· · ·

We also tried to give the players a lot more than that too, including a ton of positive reinforcement. The caveat here is that praise is only effective when it's sincere. Numbers help. If you want to praise your people for making progress, you start by measuring it. Just the measuring itself often enhances performance — and if you don't believe me, check your frequent flier miles. The mere act of keeping track affects behavior.

Example: After our first winter season, we played the first game of our ten-game summer season against the league's weakest team, but we were still tied 2–2 after two periods. If we couldn't beat those guys, we were in for a rough summer. But what really bothered me was our passive play. We weren't body-checking anyone (which is completely legal if done correctly).

Since I didn't think we had much of a chance to win the league anyway, I told our players, "Look, I don't care about the score. I don't care if we lose. But dammit, you have to hit to play hockey, and we're not hitting anyone. So for the last period, I'm not going to keep track of anything *but* hits. Now go out there and *hit some-one.*"

They did. When I started writing down the number of every player each time they made a body check, all of a sudden we were a different team, hitting everyone in sight. The energy of the game changed too, and just like that we started taking the play to our opponents. Even though I'd assumed the game was already slipping away, and with it any chance to win the title, we scored five unanswered goals to win, 7–2.

How? Instead of trying to fix a half-dozen problems we focused on one thing, we kept track of it, and we got better at it very quickly — and then everything else began to fall into place. As you might recall, we ended up winning that summer league — our first trophy in eons. Needless to say, we continued to keep stats on hits, we added stats on pancakes (knocking an opponent on his butt), and it worked like a charm for years.

I gained a related insight when I was speaking at a conference in Santiago, Chile. The speaker before me was a researcher who discovered that high achievers like being evaluated, and low achievers don't. Not too shocking, perhaps, but we too often fail to respond to what that means: If high achievers like being evaluated and low achievers don't, what should managers do? Evaluate! Measure everything you can, share it as soon as you can, and the high achievers will love it. The low achievers won't, so they'll either become high achievers, or transfer where they can be low achievers in peace.

We tracked dozens of measures before we even got on the ice, including stats for everything we did in the weight room and on the track, individually and as a team. In other words, their efforts mattered, even when no one was watching us. Once the season started, we kept track of fifteen different statistics for every player for every game, including goals and assists, shots on net, face-offs won and lost, blocked shots, and yes, hits and pancakes — and anything else that we felt contributed to winning hockey games.

All of these metrics had an immediate, positive impact, partly because they gave everyone something to shoot for and a pat on the back when they came through. Importantly, because we never told them which stats were most important, we sent another message: *they all are.* The defensemen, who rarely scored, especially loved it.

"When we started measuring all sorts of stats," assistant coach Pete Uher explains, "they started to pay more attention to other parts of their game. If you can't score a bunch of goals, you can still contribute by blocking a shot, checking someone, or winning a face-off."

The more you measure, the more you motivate.

They knew all those things were valued by their coaches and teammates because we measured them and posted the stats. We thought these measures were so important that we had a handful of reserve taxi players chart these stats for each game. Silver lining: charting stats forced the reserve players, usually freshmen, to watch the games more carefully. It also made them minor heroes when their teammates read their stats. Their work mattered.

After everyone had gone home, Uher and I would work in the coaches' room for a couple of hours pumping all the raw data into our spreadsheets. Then we'd post the results on the first wall the players saw when they walked in for practice the next day.

We didn't have to tell them to look at the posted spreadsheets. We didn't have to tell them those stats were significant. We didn't have to tell them where their play was strong and what they needed to work on. We didn't have to push them, get mad, or punish anyone for the results. The numbers alone worked — and the crowd around that spreadsheet told me those numbers mattered to them too.

What works in high school hockey will work in your organization, whether you're keeping track of sales, attendance, clicks, clients, billable hours, or whatever metrics determine your team's performance. Start keeping track of all aspects of performance, make it as public and transparent as you can, and your people will start getting better at those things without you having to say anything. Everyone on our team — and I mean *everyone* — saw those stats and made the decision to improve their game.

This tells us something else: even people who have been dismissed as notoriously low achievers probably have the basic instinct and desire for high achievement inside them. It's our job to get it out — and it's not that hard. Treat your people like high achievers and you'll be amazed how quickly they start acting like it.

We also installed plenty of team incentives to keep them going. Our second season I printed a large paper tablet with a huge number on each page, counting from 0 to 24, to keep track of our wins. Every time we won, we'd tear one page off.

I made another tablet with one page for every Huron hockey team's record, running from the worst to the best. If we won our first game, for example, we'd tear off "1999–2000: 0-22-3." Every time we passed a team's win total, we'd tear off that year.

I posted these tablets in the locker room, high above our team stereo, so you needed a chair to reach them, and I never tore off a page myself. After a win we always picked someone who had done something important — always a nice mix of stars and second-tier players — to tear the next sheet off. If we passed a few previous Huron teams that night, we could pick more guys to do the honor — and honored they were, sometimes getting choked up as their teammates cheered for them. Everyone yelled when the honoree spiked the sheet on a gold spindle against the wall, as if he were collecting scalps. We celebrated all victories, great and small.

You may think this is pretty corny, and maybe it is. But believe me: it works.

If I were running a business, I'd do the same thing: track the most important statistics and key performance indicators, list all the team's past performances we're trying to beat, and honor hardworking employees by inviting them to tear off each number we passed. I'd do it for the same reason too: to avoid drifting through each day, going through the motions, with no goals, no deadlines, no markers to shoot for, and no achievements to celebrate. That's exactly what most employees face every day when they arrive at work.

Boredom is poison. The antidote: measurable milestones.

We didn't just throw numbers at the players. We also gave them a ton of attention, praise, and reinforcement, individually and as a team. I knew their names from day one, and the other coaches connected with them quickly too. Then we all learned as much about each player as we could. This served as an important counter to all the evaluating: our interest in them had nothing to do with their achievements and everything to do with their inherent worth as human beings. Who wouldn't want more of that?

We were undeniably demanding, but we were also generous with praise. Now, I know leaders today often complain about modern employees' appetite for approval — but *why?* Praise is easy to give, it makes the recipient feel good, it makes *you* feel good, and it reinforces the behaviors you want. I don't know anything that motivates people more than praising them sincerely, in front of their peers — and it's *free*. Is there a hidden downside to praising them? None that I can see.

Praise to me is like gratitude: you only give it *after* you've already been given something. This is the best deal going. They pay you up front. Being grateful should be the easiest thing in the world.

Likewise, successful leaders don't become positive after they become successful. They learn to be positive *before* they become successful. The success follows.

The Dalai Lama said, "If you want to make someone feel better, show compassion. If you want to make yourself feel better, show compassion."

It's the same with praise. The people you praise feel better, you feel better, and behaviors and performance improve dramatically. There is no downside.

Praise is especially important for those who usually don't get to hear it: not your star performers, but the newbies, the bottom-halfers, the unsung heroes. The stars get all kinds of positive feedback from their statistics, their paychecks, the recognition they receive, but it's the ones behind the scenes who need it most. So give it to them!

When we took over the team, we had so many old habits to shake and new ones to develop that whenever I saw the slightest bit of evidence that a player or the team had a healthy new habit sprouting, I all but drowned them in lavish praise. I also made sure everyone else was alerted to this development too — not only to reinforce the new behavior but to let them all know: *This is what we want! When you do it, you will get praised for it too — publicly.*

Another old saw: catch your people doing good. I tried to give as little attention as possible to the mistakes and as much as possible to the successes.

Whatever you feed grows, so don't feed the weeds. Feed the flowers.

• • •

Another common complaint regarding today's workers is that "they just want to have fun." Well, who doesn't? Obviously no serious endeavor is going to be fun all the time. But it *has* to be fun at least some of the time, or you're going to lose them.

I had a recurring thought: *If we don't have fun, they're gonna run.* And another, from my unforgettable grade school teacher, Mr. Pudduck: "We're fair and fun and we get it done." Not a bad place to start.

My players were giving me everything I wanted—effort, engagement, team spirit—so I gave them what *they* wanted: a great locker room, team dinners, and fun, fast-paced practices with no sitting down or waiting in line. They *moved.*

This is also my answer to teachers who say, "It's not our job to entertain them." Actually, *it is*—and the best teachers always do. In all my years of teaching, coaching, and public speaking, I can't recall a single audience member walking out of a class or conference saying, "That lecture was incredibly boring, but I sure learned a lot!"

That's why, whenever I could, I swapped lectures for stories. Stories are more interesting, they connect the listener to something bigger, and they were especially effective for communicating my vision to the team without giving them a ten-minute soliloquy. I expressed my ambitions for the program through stories about Michigan football, the "Miracle on Ice" US Olympic hockey team, Muhammad Ali and George Foreman's "Rumble in the Jungle," and the time I finally managed to punch my big brother square in the nose.

I assumed they would remember those stories better than lectures, because when they were having fun, they were engaged. When your people are engrossed, they're learning, and they'll come back for more.

"You wanted to go to the workouts to hear about the vision, so you could dream about the role you could play in it," Stevie Wasik recalls. "When you are constantly hearing stories about greatness, you start to believe you are capable of more."

No matter how hard or discouraging things got, we made it a

point to have some fun every single day, with the locker room serving as home base. We had little competitions during practice, we had nicknames for everyone, and we kept a lot of inside jokes running among us — all signs of a healthy, trusting culture.

On one of our bus rides, Scooter McConnell remembers, "Bacon was talking with a few of us about the men's league team he played on with our assistant coaches. Pete Uher [pronounced "You're"] was clearly one of the most naturally talented guys on the ice, and I made the rather obvious observation, 'Uher's so damn good.'

"Bacon seemed a little surprised and said, 'Why, thank you, Scooter.'

"'No, no, no,' I explained. 'Not *you* are so damn good. Pete *Uher* is so damn good.' I probably should have just let Bacon have the compliment, since he decided who played and who didn't. It was a long time before he let me live that down."

As you can see, I still haven't. But it was good for a laugh.

Once they made the team, the players got a lot of gear, all of it with our famed Huron "H" on it — a cool logo the Balfour ring company designed with a flame atop a stylized "H" — and their jersey number on everything. The Huron "Flaming H" made it clear they were part of an elite team, and their number made it theirs.

We made the first day they walked into our locker room such a big deal that the players started calling it "Hockey Christmas." Coaches Lapper, Ned, and I, with a ton of help from the parents, filled each stall with all the new stuff they had just earned — and I do mean *earned* — with new uniforms for home games, away games, and practice; gray shorts and T-shirts for warm workouts and black fleece sweat suits for cold ones, complete with special hats and gloves; plus new hockey gloves, helmets, and a shiny name plaque atop each stall.

At our first parents' meeting, I wore a green shirt, a gold tie, and khaki pants I had bought the night before at the mall. I couldn't make them buy that stuff—the economic range of our families ran the gamut, with a few families secretly "on scholarship"—but I did suggest to them that it would be nice if the guys could wear a decent shirt and tie for big games.

After the meeting, one mom went straight to the mall and ransacked every clothing store in it—then the next mall, and the next, until she had rustled up an astounding forty matching forest green button-down shirts and "old gold" ties, all of which she dropped off at the rink in a row of bags before practice the next day. The outfits made our players feel like they were part of something special, and they inspired a phrase: "Strong and bold in green and gold!" I probably repeated that a million times, until everyone else was repeating it too.

Memphis's Peabody Hotel is known for its marching ducks, and Seattle's Pike Place Market is famous for its vendors throwing huge salmon past their customers. The Ann Arbor Huron River Rats became known for our green shirts and gold ties, with black fleece jackets and khaki pants. When we entered a rink, we made an impression, and we loved seeing heads turn.

"Deion Sanders famously said, 'You look good, you feel good. You feel good, you play good,'" Beltran recalls. "Little things like the gray workout clothes, green shirts and gold ties, and new uniforms all helped boost morale and made Huron hockey feel special. It was something you wanted to be a part of."

All this made them feel cool, like they were part of an exclusive "gang," if you will, around the school and around town. You wanted to *stay* in that gang. So you had to keep earning it, and you had to wear it the right way—and there was a right way to wear all of it. But it was up to the *seniors*, not me, to make sure their teammates looked right, whether working out, practicing, or getting off the team bus.

This may seem like silly teenage stuff—but I'm not so sure about that. Why do you still have that tattered T-shirt from the marathon you ran a decade ago? Names on the door, plaques, titles, parking spots, and fancy business cards motivate adults more than they like to admit. Some of the companies I admire most produce an array of shirts, pullovers, vests, and the like that employees can buy on their website—and they do. These companies give away a lot too, whether they're launching a new initiative or rewarding achievements. When someone earns a logo down vest for becoming a vice president, you can count on them wearing that vest the next day, no matter how warm it is.

If you want your people to feel connected to your team, the baubles help—whether it's T-shirts and hats for hockey players or special laptops, high-back chairs, company watches, or exotic vacations for your employees. It all comes with expectations they must meet, however, and it's fair game to remind them of it.

Don't underestimate how much your people care about these little gestures—and how they can motivate behavior. That, in turn, will build your culture.

Something everyone from high school hockey players to middle-aged managers needs is recommendation letters. You want a letter for college admissions? I'll write you the best damn letter I can. But I have to mean every word of what I write.

So when Ross Gimbel came to me asking for a letter, I made him a deal.

During tryouts my first year, Ross's sophomore season, it was obvious he was one of the best players out there. I couldn't believe it when he told me he'd been cut the year before. But he was dragging so much that I told him: "You're one of the best players here, but if you don't pick up your pace, you're not going to make it." He didn't pick it up, so after tryouts I put him on the taxi squad instead of the varsity.

"I was very upset," Ross recalls. "But I put my head down and decided I would do whatever was necessary to make the team and get playing time."

That's just what Ross did, and we bumped him up to varsity before our first game. But after practice one day, when I was trying to address the entire team, Ross took his hockey glove off, grabbed it by the string, and started spinning it around. When I asked him to stop, he gazed at me and said, as sarcastically as possible, "Oh okay!" Then he spun his glove around a few more times to make his point — whatever that was.

I finished my talk, then sent everyone inside. But my anger expanded too quickly, so I grabbed a black practice jersey — designated for taxi players — and marched back into the locker room. I yanked Ross's green second-line jersey out of his stall and tossed the black one at him in front of the entire team — something I never did. I was white-hot pissed, and now the whole team knew it.

On rare occasions, when your anger is organic and earned, I don't think it's a bad thing for them to see you're passionate, you have your limits, and you're not afraid to be the bad guy. You can be certain of this: everybody will remember it.

Ross never apologized, but he seemed repentant over the next few days — not his natural posture. Over the next few weeks, with assistant coach Pete Uher guiding him, Ross worked his way back into my good graces and finished the season in solid standing. We never had another problem.

Ross's junior year he was our third-highest scorer, and he emerged as a quiet leader. He did everything the right way, he was driven, and he never put himself ahead of the team. On a squad with a growing number of stars, that was a helpful combination.

"I didn't say much," Ross recalls, "but when I did, people listened, and I think that's because they were drawn to my character once they got to know me."

All true. So when Ross's teammates didn't vote him one of our captains at the outset of his senior year — mainly because we had an overabundance of good leaders — he was hurt. But, he remembers, "I used this as motivation to fuel me through the season. I wanted to prove that I was a leader of this team."

While most of our captains were vocal, emotional leaders, Ross prided himself on having a calm, levelheaded demeanor. This gave us good balance, which was especially valuable during tight games. Ross became a real force in the locker room, someone the younger players all respected.

So when Ross asked me for a college recommendation letter in the fall of his senior year, I was happy to entertain his request. But I told him, "If I write your letter right now, it will be good, but not as good as it could be, or should be. You want a great letter, one that stands out, and I want to write you one.

"So here's what you're going to do: For the next month, you're going to be on your best behavior. You're going to work hard, support your teammates, and be a leader in everything you do. I'm not asking you to be someone you're not, a yeller or a screamer. I'm asking you to be your best self. Basically, this is your chance to show me the person you want me to write about — and that's just what I'll write. Deal?"

"Deal."

If I were writing annual performance reviews, I'd do the exact same thing: bring my employee into my office two or three months before I filled out their review, tell them where they stood now, and where I wanted them to be in a few months when I actually completed it, then let them strive to make that a reality. Everybody wins.

Ross more than kept up his end of the bargain. I not only wrote him a glowing letter, explaining how he had grown into someone you could count on, I also recommended him to Al Clark, along with three other players, to become postgraduate players at Culver — "fifth-year seniors" who go to school for one year to raise their stock in the hopes of playing college hockey.

Ross was still not a great tryout player, so I was relieved when he made Culver's "A" team. He validated Clark's decision at a prestigious Boston tournament where Ross earned Most Valuable Player. He enrolled at Tufts University, where his teammates voted him MVP and — far more impressively to me — team captain his senior year. Ross had confirmed everything I'd said about him in my letter and then some, completing his journey from underestimated outsider to respected leader at the center of his team.

In the words of Mike Henry, "What an incredible story that guy is."

Ross now lives with his wife and two kids in Boston, where he's the facilities manager for sixteen Equinox high-end fitness clubs. A leader to the core, Ross is now helping his people become leaders too. When I'm in town, we get together to share a few beers, swap some old stories, and get an update on his progress—always the highlight of my trip.

I work hard for you, you work hard for me. It's a deal you can live with.

Because I'd never scored a goal at Huron, I always did my best to make sure that every player on our team scored at least once before they graduated. With the team improving every year, that usually took care of itself.

When someone scored their first goal, we followed a protocol: One of his teammates on the ice would fish the puck out of the net or ask the ref for it. We never wanted the guy who scored to have to do this. As I wrote in our game program, in a two-page spread covering "Huron Hockey Traditions": "If you see a Huron player ask the referee for the puck after a Huron goal, then hand it to one of the coaches for safekeeping, chances are it's because one of his teammates just scored his first goal. After the game the coaches write the details of the goal on the puck with a permanent gold marker, and present it to the player while his teammates cheer his accomplishment. Starting in 2000–01, every Huron player has scored at least one goal before graduating."

But as we neared the end of our second season together, we were in danger of breaking that streak. Every senior had bagged a goal except Scotty McConnell, aka "Scooter McGee," a beloved fourth-line grinder who looked like a paperboy in a Norman Rockwell painting—possibly the happiest person I've ever coached. He never complained, he always worked hard and supported his teammates, and he was so quick to laugh at just about anything, it became a running joke.

Once we put Nate Reichwage in net, we went on a roll. So with a half-dozen games left, whenever we were ahead by a few goals I'd put our two best forwards, Frags and Hairball, on the ice with Scooter, with strict instructions: "You two are *not* to shoot the puck, or even think of shooting. Just pass, pass, pass to Scooter. Got it?"

"Got it."

"Good!"

I gave Scooter equally clear instructions: "You are not to check anyone, play defense, or pass. You are to plant your butt in front of their net and shoot when these guys feed you the puck. Just shoot shoot shoot. Got it?"

"Got it."

"Good! Now go get yourself a goal."

I certainly can't defend this unorthodox approach as a strategy, but it created the desired result: lots of great chances for Scooter, with the entire team and eventually our fans pulling for him. But after a few weeks he still didn't have a goal to show for it.

"At first, I wanted to score just to get it over with," Scooter recalls, "but as we got down to the last couple games, and I saw how much my teammates were working to get me the puck, it felt like it would be as much an accomplishment for them as for me and I wanted to do my part."

For our last regular-season game, on Senior Night, we played Dexter, a smaller school nearby that had already won nineteen games that year, compared to our thirteen wins. We dressed all ten seniors that night, and our guys dominated Dexter, doing just about everything you could hope for on a Senior Night.

Ahead 5–0 halfway through the third period, we went to our Scooter Plan, putting our two stars on the ice to set him up. But once again, nothing went in. Frags and Hairball returned to the bench with about thirty seconds left, exhausted.

"We did all we could, Coach," Frags said.

"I know you did," I said, tapping them on their helmets.

But while we were talking, Scooter stayed on the ice. When a Dexter player tried to bring the puck up with ten seconds left, Scooter somehow stole the puck and skated toward their net, alone, and whacked the puck. It hit the goalie's stick and bounced right back to Scooter. He whacked it again — and *bang!* The referee blew his whistle and pointed toward the net. *Goal!*

Our guys jumped up and down, hugged and high-fived each other like we'd just won a playoff game in overtime. Our trainer Rod Sorge ran down to give me a hug.

"I didn't know you could jump that high!" he said.

"I didn't either!" I said.

"Scooter's goal was one of my favorites," Elmo recalls. "He had so many good chances and finally slammed it home. The team erupted on the bench. I mean *erupted.*"

Even the fans, who had been watching us try to set up Scooter for a month, exploded. The scoreboard said: Dexter 0. Huron 6. 00:03.2 seconds left. He'd done it!

We got the puck, and after we finished shaking hands we took a bunch of photos with the seniors, who formed a circle in the center and kissed the ice — another good sign.

"There weren't a lot of dry eyes among the senior class," Scooter says.

Then we returned to the locker room. We had just won our fourteenth game that year, passing three more teams to become Huron's second-best in thirty-four years. We tore off three sheets. Only the playoffs remained.

Then I said, "Is that it? Oh yes, we have another little bit of business!"

The locker room rumbled. They were waiting for it.

"A first goal, by none other than Scooter McGee! Come on down, Scooter!"

The same kid who couldn't stop laughing was now the only one crying.

Scooter and I were the last to leave the locker room that night. Our first year Mike Henry had started a tradition after home games for the parents, and now for friends, classmates, and actual fans too: wait in the lobby at the top of the steps to give each player a standing ovation as he walked up. Some of the guys liked it so much they found an excuse to go back to our locker room downstairs so they could climb up the stairs again.

Scooter and I walked up so much later than everyone else that I assumed the lobby would be empty, but the crowd had been waiting patiently to give Scooter the biggest cheer of all. He smiled and cried and hugged his parents.

When Scooter and I walked to the parking lot together, I put my arm around him and said, "Scooter, you will never forget this night — and neither will I!"

"Coach, I want you to know: I'm not crying because I scored. I'm crying because it's over."

- Never expect your people to work harder or to care more than you do. So be sure to do everything you ask of them at least as well as you want them to do it.

- It's fair to ask your people to give a lot to be part of your team, but you need to give them back even more in terms of time, attention, praise, support, and even swag.

- Praise works best when backed by quantifiable progress. Measure everything you can so even the unsung heroes have data to prove their value, and everyone's good habits are reinforced.

- Everyone watches how you treat the "lesser performers" on your team. If you make sure to celebrate their successes too, *everyone* feels better and works harder.

9

―――

Listen to Their Problems Now
— or You'll Get More Later

- When your people bring you their problems, questions, or ideas, *thank them.*

- Instead of replying, "No, we can't, because . . ." try, "Yes, we can, *if . . .*"

- When *you* have a problem with someone, you have two options: tell them or shut up. Anything else makes it worse.

I'm convinced that almost every problem an organization has can be boiled down to a personnel problem.

Got technology issues? Your company might have hired the wrong people, or not enough of them, or trained them poorly, or managed them ineffectively, or lost too many to turnover — or all of the above. Fix the people, you fix the problem.

If you have human beings in your organization, you're going to have problems, because they're going to have problems. We can break these down into *their* problems and *your* problems.

Let's start with their problems.

When your people bring you their problems, concerns, questions, suggestions, or ideas, instead of moaning about it, *thank them!*

We all have problems, and when we do, what do we do about them? We seek out the person we think has the most compassion, the most wisdom, and possibly the most power to help us make things right. So if a subordinate picks you to confide in, they're giving you a great compliment on several levels.

Like former secretary of state Colin Powell said, "When your people quit bringing you their problems, you quit being their leader."

To be that leader, you have to keep your door open. Whenever someone has the guts to walk through it and unload whatever's on their mind, you can't watch the clock, tell them to hurry it up, or ask them to come back another time. If they couldn't sleep the night before, you might get only one chance to help them. Blow them off, and they may never come back.

No, it's probably not the "best time." You have pressing work on your mind, deadlines aplenty, and I can virtually guarantee that their visit won't be convenient. Well, this is what you're paid for. As they say, life is what happens when you're making other plans.

If you pass up your chance to help your employee, they'll seek out someone else, and then *that* person becomes their leader. Or worse, they'll just leave, without telling you why — but they will most likely tell their friends and colleagues.

Sometimes what they want will be pretty simple, like working a different shift, with different coworkers, or in a different department. In our case, the players' most common request was to play with different line-mates. (In ice hockey, players are organized in four "lines" for the forwards, with each line consisting of a left wing, center, and right wing, and usually three pairs of defensemen consisting of left and right. Most coaches play at least three lines of forwards in every game.)

For me these requests cut both ways. If I immediately granted every request to change line-mates, those requests would quickly multiply and our game lineup would have no stability. But if I ignored every such request, my players would conclude that I never listened or cared and they'd stop bringing me their ideas and insights.

I told my team I'd handle such requests like Santa Claus: asking for what you want is no guarantee you'll get it, but I would be a fool not to take your requests seriously. Otherwise, no one gets what they want and then everyone's unhappy.

So here's what I would do when a guy came into my office to request a line change. First, I'd make sure the door was closed so no one outside got their feelings hurt. No one likes to hear that their line-mate wants to switch. Then I'd ask him why he wanted to change. What benefits would the *team* receive for making this switch? Why would the new lines be better than what we had already?

If he couldn't give any better answers than, "We're friends," or "I think he's cool," the request died right there. But if he could give me tangible reasons, I would tell him, "Okay, I'll consider it. No guarantees, though — and the lines stay the same this week. Doing your best now puts me in a better mood to consider your request next week." Unspoken message: sabotaging your current line won't help you or the team.

But after the meeting I'd keep my word: I'd take a closer look at our lines during practices and games, I'd consult with the assistants, and I'd seriously consider the change. And last, if I concluded the switch might have merit, I'd talk to the other players who'd be affected — telling them this was *my* idea, not their line-mates'.

"What would you think if I swapped out Keith for Chris on your line?"

Sometimes the other players liked the idea as much as the player who asked for it, and when that happened, we were golden. Then I'd bring in the player who made the request and tell him, "I think you might be right. But the proof will be in the pudding. You have one week to show me. If it doesn't work, we'll go back to what we had."

There's a well-known psychological phenomenon called the

Hawthorne Effect: almost any change in our work routines will improve production, at least for a while, even if it's as mundane as painting the walls of your factory, changing the coffee break times, or replacing the chairs. Although results from such experiments haven't always backed the hypothesis, I can tell you that whenever we made a player-requested line change, it almost always worked, to everyone's benefit. I still believe the main reason it worked was not because of any chemistry the switch magically unleashed, but because of their desire to make it work. If your people know they've been heard, you've accepted their idea, and now they have to prove they were right — well, believe me, you've got motivated troops.

So, whenever possible, instead of responding to ideas or requests with the usual, "No, we can't, because . . ." try to offer, "Yes, we can, *if* . . ." By adding a condition, you'll learn if they're committed to their idea. If they are, not only do you get inspired workers, but you can also get something you want from them out of the deal.

Likewise, when a player had an idea, big or small, we always heard them out and often implemented it. Now, some players had more ideas than we could handle. One of our star players, Pete "Hairball" Heeringa, offered a dozen ideas every game. Pete was probably the smartest, most observant player I've ever coached, so it's not surprising that I agreed with most of his suggestions, and we acted on many of them.

But occasionally it seemed appropriate to remind Hairball of what our roles actually were. After receiving his fifth suggestion during the first period of a game, I might say with a grin, "Tell you what, Hairball: how about *I* try coaching the team tonight, and see how that goes?"

Pulling him back once in a while was fair game, and Hairball took it well. But shutting him down and discouraging him from speaking his mind would have cost us a lot of motivation, engagement, and, not least, good ideas. And he had a lot of them!

Another bonus: listening to your people turns them into allies. Scattered throughout your team, allies can tell you what's really happening. They know better than you do where the points of friction are. If you have a question, now you have someone you can ask who knows you, knows the situation, and owes you a favor.

You hear all the time that communication is the key to success in any endeavor, whether in business or sports. That's what we're talking about here. The very best leaders listen to what their people are saying, for the simple reason that it's important.

Jim Hackett played football at Michigan before becoming CEO of Steelcase Furniture, then Michigan's athletic director, and finally Ford Motor Company's CEO. He explained to me why he instituted his surprising open-door management policy. In addition to his desire to serve his people and help them all he can, he said, "how do you think I know what the heck is going on around here? They tell me!"

Sometimes helping your people with *their* problems can solve some of yours too.

We entered our second season with high expectations, but as I've said, a battle between our two starting goalies caused both to play far below their abilities — until we gave Nate Reichwage a chance. His surprising success changed our outlook literally overnight.

But that wasn't the only issue we had to resolve. After splitting our first two games, we were an unsettled team when we traveled to Muskegon, Michigan, for a Thanksgiving tournament. We had reason to be apprehensive. Huron had gotten trounced in its two previous Thanksgiving tournaments, and we suspected we had been invited back to be the "tournament punching bag," in Elmo's words. But we won the first game 5–0, and in the finals we dismantled our foes, 10–1, to claim another trophy.

But then we kept stumbling as the season progressed, playing a good game one night then blowing it the next. Goaltending aside, we had yet to gel as a team.

Things came to a head after a 6–3 victory at Chelsea. As I wrote later that night to the players and parents, captain Chris Kunkel "decided to meet with the other players, then meet with the coaches to discuss a number of concerns and improvements we could make, on and off the ice."

When Kunkel first gathered the seniors in the stands of our rink, Scooter McConnell recalls, "I thought he was going to say we needed to work harder and play better as a team. Instead, he opened it up by saying we should talk about what we wanted to see done differently, and he'd go first: 'I don't want to hear another word about last year's team.' We talked for a while and then agreed that the seniors would meet with Coach Bacon to bring up our concerns.

"We told [Bacon] that the comparisons to last year's team were making it harder for us to feel like this was our team and our season. We also asked if we could have our weekly study table at the rink, instead of having to drive back across town to our school. There were one or two other changes we wanted made, but that was about it."

There are a lot of ways to respond when your people meet privately and then bring you requests like that, including paranoia, anger, and defensiveness. Those reactions are all guaranteed to make the situation much worse and might even spark a mutiny. Instead, I considered the fact that Kunkel had already established himself as a superb captain, one who had the complete trust of the coaches and players alike and who would never bring me requests if he wasn't serious. Everything they were asking for was reasonable, wouldn't cost us anything, and would make us better. Further, I'd been pushing Kunkel to be a more vocal, active leader, and guess what? This was exactly what that looks like: recognizing problems, speaking up for his teammates, and having the guts to approach me.

So I listened without interruption. I readily agreed to all the seniors' requests, and then, as Scooter recalls, "[Bacon] said, 'I've been waiting for you guys to do this. This is the kind of leadership that's going to make us successful.'"

I reported to our players and parents in my email later that night: "The meeting was one of the best examples of maturity, responsibility, and leadership I've seen — and one of the most signifi-

cant developments of this season, on or off the ice, dwarfing the results of the game itself."

We blew out our next Metro League opponent, 9–4, split two
close games, started Nate Reichwage in net against Grosse Pointe
South, then went on a roll that took us right up to the playoffs with a
14-8-2 record, already second-best in school history, and with win-
nable playoff games remaining. But I believe none of that would
have happened if our captain hadn't felt secure enough to meet privately with the seniors and the rest of the team, bring me their concerns, and feel confident they would be heard, respected, and taken
seriously.

If someone has the courage to tell you what their problems are,
you better have the courage to listen. Besides, why wouldn't you
want to help them? If you can do it, your people will make sure you
won't regret it.

Sometimes listening to your people means you have to hear some
things you'd rather not, especially when they're about mistakes *you*
made. But that's when listening is most important.

In terms of on-ice goals, nothing meant more to us than beating
our archrival, Ann Arbor Pioneer. On the morning of June 15, 2001,
when I was just starting to wake up but had not yet opened my eyes,
this thought popped into my head, unbidden: *We play Pioneer in
exactly six months.* You could say this game weighed heavily on me.

The Pioneer coach is the same age as I am, and a lifelong friend.
But during game week we had a gentleman's agreement: even
though our locker rooms were only ten feet apart, we would not
talk to each other — and we passed each other in the hallway several
times each day. A nod was all we offered, if that, and it was mutu-
ally understood.

The arena would be overflowing with two thousand excited fans,
and the *Ann Arbor News* would give the game a big play. Ramping

up to the December 15, 2001, showdown, we were having a slightly better season than Pioneer, a program that had once won two state titles and was often ranked in the top ten. A lot of folks thought that this was our year to beat Pioneer for the first time in four seasons — and I was one of them.

The Pioneers were good, but our guys made it clear from the opening face-off that they were in fact the better team. We were beating them to the loose pucks, hitting them every chance we had, and keeping the puck in their end most of the night. We outshot them 31–13 — a dominant performance. But thanks to some hot goaltending at their end and some shaky goaltending at ours, before Nate had taken over the position, we lost, 4–3.

We were devastated. I felt like I'd just swallowed a grenade — and I'm sure I wasn't alone. But our players had worked hard and supported each other to the hilt. I couldn't have asked for more. In the locker room I told our guys how proud I was of them, how they'd proved they were the better team, and that I'd never trade any of them for one of our rivals across the hallway. I meant every word too.

A heartbreaking setback like that sucks more energy out of you than getting blown out in a lopsided loss. But to make matters even worse, I had also broken a promise I had made to the players at the outset of our first season: if you're wearing green, you're getting in the game. Yes, I'd been up-front that playing time would not be equal — if you wanted that, you could join the local rec league — but that unlike high school teams that routinely did not play all their players, at Huron we would get every player into every game they dressed for.

Entering the third period, I still needed to get a couple of guys in. I wasn't afraid they'd screw up, but everything was working so well, and we seemed so close to breaking the game open, that I kept putting off making any changes. With a couple of seconds left, when I finally accepted that we couldn't win, I also realized I had broken my promise. I quietly approached both players I failed to get into the game afterward to apologize, but that still didn't make it right.

The next day one of them, Adam Was — a senior who had worked his tail off, supported his teammates, and done everything we'd asked of him — reached out to me to talk about the situation. We agreed to meet at a local restaurant that night at 10 p.m., when I would finally be free. I admit I was bone-tired after a draining week, but I'd already broken one promise that week, and I didn't feel like breaking another. Adam was measured and reasonable, but understandably hurt and confused. This case was simple: he was right, and I was wrong. I apologized sincerely and promised him I wouldn't make the same mistake again, and I didn't.

The lesson: when you screw up — and you will — admit it, apologize, and *fix it* as best you can. Former Michigan athletic director Don Canham once told me, "Never turn a one-day story into a two-day story." Politicians, business leaders, and others fail that test when they lack the humility to admit they're wrong, and the confidence to believe they can take the hit and survive it.

I was fortunate that I was at Adam's mercy. He graciously accepted my *mea culpa*, kept working hard and supporting his teammates, and, as we so often said, "finished strong." But even if I had broken my promise to someone less mature and understanding, my response should have been no different, no matter the cost. As Martin Luther King Jr. once said, "The time is always right to do what is right."

Adam went on to graduate from MIT, where he starred on the hockey team, and then from Harvard Medical School. One year he came down to our Huron High School alumni game and told me, "Looking back, it wasn't about the playing time, but the experience and the lessons."

That was a generous gift he certainly didn't owe me, one I will never forget.

In the spring of 2020, after COVID postponed the Boston Marathon, I created my own marathon around my hometown and invited my friends on social media to join me — at a safe distance, of course. I was pleasantly surprised to be joined by Dr. Adam Was for a few miles. When I told him how much it meant to me, he said,

"My pleasure, Coach — but don't flatter yourself. Thanks to COVID, you're the only game in town."

I let him have the last word. He'd earned it.

Now let's talk about *your* problems.

We've all been criticized to our faces, and we've all been criticized behind our backs. Neither one tickles, but which one feels worse? Not even close, is it?

No one likes being criticized. But if your boss does it privately, to your face, you can still trust her. You might even gain respect for her over time for bringing it directly to you and not going to someone else. I've found that when I criticize someone directly and privately, they'll usually resent me for a day, then slowly warm up until, by the end of the week, our relationship is stronger than it was before I challenged them. In fact, many of the players I'm closest to now are the same ones I had confronted years earlier. When you face a moment of truth together, it often serves as the basis for a stronger relationship.

But when you hear about someone criticizing you behind your back, that sting doesn't go away. From that moment on, you can never look at that person the same way, and you will never give them your wholehearted effort again, either.

This one's easy to prove: We can all remember when someone we respected told us privately that our work wasn't cutting it. After, that we worked harder to avoid letting that mentor down. Those leaders often became our favorite teachers, coaches, and bosses.

Conversely, everyone remembers someone we considered a trusted ally talking behind our backs, forever fracturing our relationship. I've found myself in my car at stoplights thinking about how some kid in fifth grade did me wrong — and I don't even know if he's still alive. That, my friends, represents a whole lot of wasted energy — but that's how seriously we take being betrayed, no matter how small the offense.

As I said, if you have people in your organization, you will have problems with some of them, and some of them will have problems with you. It's the price of being human, and there's no way to avoid paying it.

During one of my many calls to Al Clark, when I talked about a player who needed an attitude adjustment, Clark replied, "Well, John, if all the kids were perfect, our work wouldn't count for much."

Boom. By that measure, our work as leaders should count for a lot. Your people's mistakes, problems, and headaches do not represent some unfortunate distraction keeping you from doing your job. Those problems *are* your job.

So first things first. When you become aware of someone creating problems in your ranks, don't waste precious energy feeling like a victim, cursing the darkness, or complaining to someone else about the person in question. Those situations are why they pay you. Without them, your job would be clear sailing — and then they'd cut your salary in half or eliminate your job altogether.

Take the opposite approach. Be thankful that you've been made aware of the problem. If you hadn't been, then you'd really be screwed. Second, be grateful that you're in a position to do something about it. And third, *do something about it!*

After Elmo and I got on the same page our first year together, he had a very good season. Elmo was the best player on the team, and also one of the humblest. Our second year, when he was no longer the best player, he was one of the most supportive, jokingly calling our squad "Team Fragner," in honor of our new best player.

For all these reasons, Adam Was, the future Harvard-trained doctor, once said, "Elmo is the most beloved guy in our locker room."

After Scooter McConnell's unforgettable goal on Senior Night, we won our first playoff game. But after practice the next day, Elmo told me his girlfriend had bought him tickets for a concert in Boston for that Saturday night, the same night as the regional playoff final.

True, we would play on Saturday only if we won Thursday night, but I didn't want to dress someone Thursday night who wasn't going to be with us Saturday night.

One of the great things about principles: they make difficult decisions simpler. Faced with his dilemma, I restated the obvious: attending every practice and game was a condition of being on the team. If Elmo couldn't commit to playing in the regional final Saturday, then I wasn't going to let him play in our semifinal playoff game on Thursday.

This wasn't punishment, as I saw it. It was mere accountability. But I also told him, "Elmo, don't do this. We need you. The guys look up to you – and this would be terrible for team spirit, and a horrible way to finish after all you've come through. But, obviously, it's your call."

He said he'd think about it.

When Elmo arrived the next day, a few hours before our second playoff game, we pulled him into the coaches' room and closed the door. He said, "I've decided to stay."

I was relieved – for Elmo, and for the team.

We won our second playoff game that night, 3–1. That set up a regional final match against the mighty Trenton Trojans in their home rink – as hard as it gets.

The next morning I called Herb Brooks himself, the coach of the 1980 "Miracle on Ice" US Olympic team that beat the Soviets, the greatest upset in the history of sports. I had interviewed Herb for several stories over the previous five years, and we had become friends. We were even talking about writing a book together. The reason for my call wasn't about our book, however, but my Huron hockey team. I explained the situation to Herb, how we'd be playing the role of the upstart Americans, and Trenton the seemingly unbeatable Soviets.

I will never forget his response: "Johnny, just tell 'em this: Above all, you gotta believe. If you don't, nothing is possible. But if you do, *anything is possible.*"

After our team dinner the night before our game, I passed on Herb's message, which made a big impression on our guys. I then added, "I admit, I'm scared. But not for you guys. You guys are a runaway freight train, a team that went from zero wins to sixteen in two years. No one does that — and what's more impressive is *how* you did it. I know how hard you work, and how close you are. I know how *good* you are. But the Trojans don't know any of those things. I see you coming, but they don't. I'm not worried for you. I'm worried for *them.* They're about to get *steamrolled* — and they won't know what hit 'em.

"I don't *think* we're going to beat Trenton. I *know* we are. And you do too."

They did.

"I remember being so focused going into the game," Ross Gimbel recalls. "We were ready to beat them, finally. I could feel it. But I knew we needed a little extra kick to beat Trenton, so I let my heart out in the locker room right before the game. I told the guys exactly how I was feeling, that I believed in them, believed in the team, and let out a final roar which every teammate followed up with a scream. We were ready for battle and exploded out of the locker room onto the ice. I knew we were ready for that game, and we sure as hell played like it."

In front of a full house, we attacked from the opening face-off, showing no fear. After five minutes of fury, we scored, sending a clear message: we're not the team you crushed 13–2 the previous year. We're not here for a moral victory. We're here to *beat you.*

"For the first time [against a Trenton team], we believed in each other," captain Chris Kunkel remembers. "Through the sweat, the tears, and all the time that we put into achieving our goals, we believed we were good enough to play with the best and that we deserved to win their respect and win the game."

Trenton came back with a power-play goal to tie us, 1–1, but we didn't back off, outshooting Trenton in the first period, 14–9. We had come to play. After Trenton took a 2–1 lead in the second, Chris Kwon battled for the puck along the boards and popped it out to Pat "Cosmo" Commiskey, who had snuck behind their goalie. Just like that, Cosmo recalls, "I was looking at nothing but the puck and a wide open net."

Any of us would have tapped the puck into the net as quickly as we could for a crucial goal. Not Cosmo. Years of pent-up frustration had finally found its outlet.

"Cosmo winds up!" Elmo recalls. "He *winds up! No one* does that. Watching him, everybody's butt puckered up."

Then the same guy who led the "0-and-20!" chant at the school dance just two years earlier made a very different statement, ripping the puck into the open net.

Huron 2, Trenton 2.

We didn't fear them. They feared us — and with good reason. They were in a dogfight that we were fully prepared for but they never saw coming.

The intensity never let up. Everyone on our bench stood the entire game. In the third period we went down 3–2, but we were still playing them shot for shot and hit for hit — nothing fluky about it. Complete two years of killer off-season workouts in the weight room, on the track, and against the wall, and you start to gain an advantage.

"We were the best-conditioned team that season," captain Chris Kunkel recalls. "One of my favorite memories was in the third period, lining up for a face-off and looking over at their exhausted forward, red in the face and huffing and puffing. I would smile and give him a wink because I knew he wanted to give up in fatigue."

Of course, we knew better than to think Trenton would give up against anyone, especially during a regional final in their own building, but Kunkel was right: we were pushing the best players in the state to their very limits.

"We had come a long way in two short years," Kunkel adds. "We were no longer up against untouchables anymore. We were now *ruthless* on the attack, setting up designed plays that you read about. Bing-bang-boom. We were fun to watch. No one was worried.

"We all had the sense that we just needed more time. Keep the pressure on, and the dam would break sooner or later. We were peppering their goalie, who was standing on his head for the majority of the game. Everyone believed that we were going to win. There was no other way this story was going to end."

Still down 3–2 with a minute to go, we pulled our goalie for an extra attacker and unleashed a barrage of shots on their net. We even hit the pipe, which rang out, but we just couldn't get anything to go in. When the final horn blew, Trenton had survived, 3–2.

The Trojans were visibly relieved to get out of that game alive. Their fans even gave our guys a standing ovation — one they richly deserved.

"I will never forget shaking the hand of the Trenton captain and him stopping me," Kunkel recalls. "He gave me a big hug and whispered in my ear, 'You guys should have won that game.'"

A class act from a class team.

I told my guys not to go into the locker room but to stand on our blue line while the Trojans received their medals. I went down our line, giving all our players a handshake and a message: "You belong here. You have earned this right. *Stand tall.*"

Later, in the locker room, I said, "You just outplayed the best team in the state — and everyone knows it." Then I asked them, with a glint in my eye, "Hey! What's the first rule of Huron hockey?!?"

Through tears they boomed it the first time: "*Work hard!*"

"What's the second rule?"

"*Support your teammates!*"

"That's right. You did it a year and a half ago, when they kicked our asses 13–2, you've done it every game since, and you did it again today. What was true then, is true now. *I am proud of you!* Now shower up and go see your families, your friends, your fans. I'm sure they're waiting in the lobby to cheer you when you come out."

Sure enough, Trenton's lobby was packed with our backers, including Steve Beltran himself, who made the drive to cheer us on. But no one was moved more than the guy who almost missed that game.

"I cried my eyes out after we lost to Trenton," Elmo recalls. "I didn't want to take off my jersey because I knew that this group of guys would never be in that room again."

I walked out spent, but so proud of our guys—and none more so than Elmo.

Two days later the players returned to our locker room to turn in their equipment and vote for our team awards. To give the players as much privacy as possible, the coaches always remained in our cramped office while the players filled out their ballots. So we didn't know what Elmo was up to while we waited for them to finish.

"Lapper did not do the easy thing," Elmo recalls. "He always did the right thing, and he never asked for anything in return. It was clear who deserved the Unsung Hero Award," which had been established to reward a player, not a coach.

Working with the defense for two years, Lapper helped cut our goals-against in half. On game days he made the locker room look like an NHL clubhouse. When the players arrived, they would see their pants and jerseys hanging in their stalls, their names and numbers facing out, and rolls of tape stacked in pyramids on the training table. Not least, he had kept the guys from quitting early on when they wondered what their crazy new head coach was all about. Just about every player would tell you Lapper was their biggest supporter. He loved the players, and they loved him. The best part is, both sides knew it.

Elmo told me he walked around the locker room, "tripping over legs to whisper, '*Vote for Lapp!*' But it didn't take much convincing. The team already felt the same way. I only wish that I was there to see Lapper's face when you started tallying up the votes."

The coaches took the ballots to a local pub to add them up. While we sipped our pints, I saw someone had written in Lapper's name for the Unsung Hero Award.

"Hey, Lapper, look at this! Pretty cool, eh?"

He was flattered and embarrassed, but he obviously deserved it.

"Hey look — another one!" I said, showing him a second ballot with his name on it. And another. And another. We soon realized every single player had voted for Lapper. I'd never seen anything like it.

At the senior banquet, we had a lot to celebrate. We had finished 16-9-2, the second-best record in school history. It says something about where we started that we could break the record for most improved team two years in a row.

But the emotional highlight of the night was announcing the winner of the Unsung Hero Award. When I handed Lapper the trophy, he was too choked up to speak, and too modest to look up. He just stared down at the trophy. The players got red-eyed too. It meant as much to them as it did to Lapper — maybe more.

We soon learned that the catalyst behind Lapper's unanimous selection was none other than Jon "Elmo" Eldredge. Seeing Lapper clutch that trophy, I was as proud of Elmo as I was of the young coach holding the hardware.

Elmo, the same guy who could only think of himself when debating going to Boston two weeks earlier, was now the first person to think of everyone else.

- When your people want to share an idea, a question, or a problem with you, thank them. Whenever possible, instead of replying, "No, we can't, because . . ." try, "Yes, we can, if . . ." This way, everyone gets something out of the deal.

- When you listen to your people, you not only can help them with their problems, but they can often give you insights and ideas you couldn't get from anyone else.

- When you have a problem with someone, you have two choices: either bring it to them and only them, or keep it to yourself. Doing anything else will make things worse. But if you bring the problem directly to them, you've given them their very best chance to come through.

Giving Control

10

Make Peer Pressure Work for You

- Peer pressure is here to stay, so make it work for your team.

- You need to engage both positive and negative peer pressure.

- The rules apply to you too. But if you play by them, your people won't forget it.

Whenever you hear the phrase "peer pressure," you can bet it's framed as a negative. True, peer pressure is usually a problem, as anyone whose friends coerced them into smoking, drinking, or swallowing goldfish can attest. But my belief is that peer pressure can be transformed into accountability and put to good use for your team.

I'll even go one step farther: positive peer pressure is *essential to letting your people lead*. You need to make them accountable to *each other*, not just to you.

This accomplishes two objectives at once: workers tend to feel more obligated to each other than they do to their leader, no matter who their leader is; and second, you won't burn out trying to manage everyone every minute of the day.

So how can we harness peer pressure to make it work for everyone? Once again, accountability, like character, is not an accident. You need to install sturdy systems to take advantage of peer pressure, or it will take advantage of you.

We applied peer pressure both to reinforce the positive and to diminish the negative. That started with our grueling workouts, in which we paired players to lift together in the weight room, then made everyone accountable for the *team's* time on the outdoor track. My observation of human nature tells me that we will let ourselves down far more quickly than we'll let down a teammate. With their fates tied together, the River Rats excelled. Their incredible improvement on the track, reducing the team's sprint relay time from 14:40 to 11:42 while running for each other, proves it.

The same holds true for your employees. Set up systems that require them to work together, and everyone will feel accountable for the team's success.

You should also take your workspace seriously, because where your people work can have a big impact on how your team functions.

Most teams let their players sit wherever they want, but that inevitably results in the seniors clustering in the best seats, while the freshmen fend for themselves far away — not exactly a recipe for team unity. So every fall I'd make ten copies of our locker room floor plan, with each stall clearly marked along the walls. Then I'd play around with possible seating combinations and work it like a logic game.

I knew I wanted all eight of our defensemen on our longest wall, together, and our fifteen forwards on the other three walls, with the three goalies getting the biggest stalls on the ends. But I also wanted one of my four strongest leaders in the middle of each of our four walls, like compass points, with the strongest at true north, the second on the south, the third east, and the fourth west. I wanted to avoid having two seniors sitting next to each other, or two members of any class, because it was too easy for them to hang out with guys in their grade and not get to know the others. Finally, I considered friendships, and guys I thought would be good or bad influences on each other.

I kept working this puzzle again and again, until I was satisfied that I had created the best possible seating arrangement. Before everyone arrived for their first practice, I'd put their name plaques in the metal frames above their new stalls, making it "official," and no one ever complained. It only occurs to me now that, once we set up the seating chart, we never had to move anyone, so we probably got it right.

I stole this next idea while writing a feature story on Japanese hockey for *ESPN Magazine* (inevitably titled "Puck-E-Mon"). I learned that the leading Japanese companies, including Toyota, Sony, and Panasonic, and even Japan's professional hockey teams, follow a practice called "senpai-kohai" (pronounced "sen-pie, ko-high"), or mentor-protégé, in which they pair up senior employees with junior employees to guide and advise them throughout their careers. This breaks down barriers, it instills in the senpai a sense of responsibility for the next generation, and it gives the kohai the security of having a senior employee looking out for them.

This was particularly important for our team because, unlike most high school sports, our hockey program didn't have a junior varsity until I created one our fourth year; until then, Huron hockey had just one team for everyone. So we had fourteen-year-old ninth-graders who weren't shaving yet getting dressed next to eighteen-year-old seniors who could vote and enlist in the military (as one of our seniors soon did). How do you get guys who are so far apart in age and maturity to know each other, to care about each other, and to fight for each other? You try everything you can — from a carefully constructed seating chart to senpai-kohai.

But unlike the Japanese, who rarely question the time-honored system, I knew our guys would have to like it for it to succeed. So instead of just assigning everyone a mentor or a protégé, I had both the upperclassmen and the underclassmen fill out a three-choice "wish list" of teammates they'd like to mentor or be mentored by. Then I took their ballots and worked another logic game until I had ensured that everyone was paired with one of the three people on their list. To my relief, we were always able to pull this off.

Once they were matched up, each senpai-kohai pair would sit together on the bus, eat together at team meals, room together on overnight trips, and work together in some other activities I'd throw in occasionally just to keep the senpai-kohai program strong.

I really had no idea how the guys were going to receive this, and I would've scrapped senpai-kohai if they didn't bite. But somewhat to my surprise, they didn't merely like it, they *loved* it, and they started insisting months ahead of our next season that we do it again. It worked because they felt connected and accountable to each other, and we made it fun.

To this day every player on our team can remember who their senpai or kohai was. Most are still in touch, and some have even stood up at each other's wedding.

That's how you get positive peer pressure to work for you.

We used peer pressure to correct negative behaviors too.

There are countless ways to engage negative peer pressure responsibly, and we used a few. When a player screwed up, I'd often ask the captains or seniors what they thought I should do before making my decision. Sometimes I even asked the player in question. I quickly learned that they were always tougher on themselves than I would have been — and I mean *always.*

After we worked out a fair consequence, we would often have the player address his teammates to explain what happened, apologize sincerely, and assure them that it wouldn't happen again. The idea was *not* to embarrass or humiliate the player. Quite the opposite: we wanted his teammates to see that he felt accountable to them — which would help restore their respect for him — and for him to feel the support of his teammates. Every time a player apologized, his stock rose among his peers and he benefited from their backing. It worked because it was all conducted among the players, not the coaches.

This mindset actually expanded our strategic options too. Our first year I felt compelled to follow the philosophy of former Philadelphia Flyers' head coach Fred Shero, who said, "I give my players very simple tasks, and I make them do them very, very well."

But after our guys had mastered the basics, their strong sense of discipline and accountability to each other allowed us to run complicated, aggressive, and risky systems — systems that depended on each player doing his job for the others or the whole scheme would break down. We could do this because we had complete confidence they would stick to the plan and not let each other down. They got it down so well that we could trigger a handful of plays our opponents had never seen before with just a hand signal from me on the bench. It was fun for us to do, and hard for our opponents to stop.

The same idea applies to business: the more disciplined your people are and the stronger their sense of accountability to each other, the more sophisticated the options you'll have to attack problems — options your competitors wouldn't dare consider.

Every organization is going to suffer self-inflicted wounds, and dumb penalties were ours. This bothered the hell out of me because I've never seen a team I admired take dumb penalties, and I certainly did not want to be the coach of one of those teams.

Whenever we faced an obstacle, instead of trying to attack some ill-defined blob of a problem, we tried to break it down into its various components to see if we could address those more easily. In this case, we broke down penalties into three groups: penalties that were the by-product of being a physical, aggressive team; penalties that occurred far from the puck; and penalties that were called after the whistle had already stopped play.

We defined "aggressive penalties" as infractions that resulted from contact with the puck carrier when our technique was a little off. I didn't get mad about these because we wanted to be a hungry team, and we expected our guys to be tough. This is hockey, after all, not ballet. It's a contact sport that does not reward passivity.

But we also wanted to be a clean team that played smart hockey. One of our goals every year was taking the fewest penalties in the league, and while we never quite achieved it — Trenton usually took the fewest penalties, which tells you something — we came very close each year. So when we got penalties for being aggressive, we would work on our technique the next practice with the player involved, or the entire team if necessary, to show them, for example, how to tuck their elbow in while driving their shoulder into the opponent's chest to avoid an elbowing call. But we knew that if we were going to be tough, we would take some penalties for aggressive play, which are also the most likely to be miscalled by a ref. We could live with that.

The second category, penalties away from the puck, not so much! These were usually the result of a dustup with an opponent — two guys barking at each other thirty feet behind the play and eventually jamming a stick or throwing a quick punch at each other. These penalties had nothing to do with the play itself, and they certainly had nothing to do with being smart, tough, or disciplined as we defined those things.

The third category, penalties taken after the whistle, were even worse. By definition, once the referee blows the whistle, the play is over, so you can't possibly tell me taking penalties afterward helps a team in any tangible way. The one exception here was protecting our goalie, one of hockey's unwritten rules, like protecting one's quarterback. If anyone came after our goalie, even after the whistle, they needed to be confronted — though even there we taught our players how to keep the bad guys away without taking dumb penalties, and it usually worked.

I've always thought the second and third penalty categories are generally committed by "tough guy wannabes"—players who aren't willing to hit or be hit legally, but are trying to score street cred by committing flashy but stupid penalties. In these cases it was essential that we separated being tough from being stupid, which are too often conflated. To do so, I needed only to name a few guys who everyone agreed were among the toughest guys on our team, but who took very few penalties.

"Everyone here think Jeff Marley is tough?" I'd ask, getting a lot of nods. "I agree. He's one of the toughest, most physical players in the league. Guess what? He has three penalties all year, and one of those was for protecting our goalie.

"What about Perry Merillat? Everyone think he's tough? He has one penalty—*all season*. It's not because he's backing off. It's because he plays smart, uses good technique, and never puts himself ahead of the team — nothing stupid or selfish behind the play or after the whistle. That's what we're trying to do here!"

How does this apply to the business world? Every field of endeavor rewards achievement, but also has lines that can't be crossed. You're always trying to achieve the former without incurring the latter. Trial lawyers want to win cases without being held in contempt or getting disbarred. Surgeons want successful outcomes without incurring malpractice suits. Salespeople want to break records without generating customer complaints or breaking the law.

So how do you encourage your team to achieve without setting off alarms? You want your people to see crossing the line not as an unavoidable side effect of their hard work, but as something diametrically opposed to what your team is trying to achieve. Single out the high achievers who do *not* have a history of infractions — the winning lawyer beloved by clients, the successful surgeon with a great bedside manner, the top salesperson with the high customer reviews — and that usually does the trick. But we had other techniques too.

. . .

One of our goals was to take three penalties or fewer every game. If we got into double digits, it was usually because our technique and discipline had gradually eroded until we were getting downright sloppy. Then you start turning games you should be winning into defeats.

After we took a dozen penalties one night, I was trying to think of a way to fix this problem beyond merely lecturing the players again, which was getting old for all of us. Driving home, I had an idea that I thought might be worth trying.

The next day I found the crappiest chair at the rink — a rusty old metal thing — and when practice started, I put that chair at center ice, facing us, as we stood on the goal line. I then produced a copy of the scoresheet from the previous night's game. They had no idea what I was up to, but they figured it out pretty quickly.

I started with my boilerplate speech on the difference between being tough and being stupid and selfish. I spelled out our three categories of penalties once again and underscored the responsibility they all had *to each other* to play the game the right way. Then I closed my little soliloquy by saying: "I'm done talking about it. You've heard my speech enough times to know it by heart. Everyone here knows the difference between being tough and being stupid — but I guess we've forgotten how important that is."

Then I looked at the scoresheet and read off our first penalty, committed by our best defenseman: "Number 17, Dan Sheldon, two minutes, roughing."

I told Danny to skate out to center ice and sit in the crappy chair — "with no attitude," I instructed, "like you're sitting for a freakin' team photo." Then I told everyone else, "When I blow the whistle, the rest of us are going to skate full speed all the way down to the other end, hit the glass with our sticks, then go full speed all the way back. If we don't go full speed — and I mean *everyone* going full speed, all the way — then *we all* do it again."

That was another way to instill accountability and peer pressure — and they had no reason to doubt that I meant it.

"Why do *we* have to skate?" one player asked. "Danny took the penalty!"

"Because what happens to Danny when he takes a penalty?" I asked. "He goes to the penalty box, and he sits there for two minutes by himself, while *we* have to skate with only four players against five to kill the penalty. So if we're going to have Danny on our team taking stupid penalties, apparently we're going to need to be in much better shape. The coaches are skating with you too, because if we're dumb enough to coach players who take dumb penalties, we're dumb enough to join you. So, let's go!"

I blew the whistle, and we all took off, full blast, slamming our sticks against the far glass, then skating back full blast, past the goal line. Then I motioned Danny out of the chair and called out the next penalty. That player sat in the chair, and we did it all again.

But I stress this: I was not trying to embarrass the player sitting in the chair. I was trying to get him to recognize that his actions affected everyone—and the entire team needed to realize that too: they were all accountable to each other.

The first few sprints they found mildly amusing, but by our fourth full-length sprint, the novelty started wearing off. The players soon got tired and frustrated hearing many of the same names called out again and again. And here's the beautiful part: *I never had to say another word.* The more we skated, the more names I called out—"Kunkel, two minutes, cross-checking"—the more glares *the players* shot the guy in the seat, the less I had to say. A few of them, even with their hockey gloves on, managed to flip the guy in the chair a half-serious middle finger on their way by. The gesture really wasn't necessary, though, because the poor guy in the chair was already feeling quite guilty just watching everyone skate sprints because of what he'd done.

After we finished our last sprint, the point had been made a dozen times over: if you're going to take stupid, selfish penalties, you're not screwing over your coaches. You're screwing over your teammates, who have to cover for you. You're accountable *to them*, not to me.

The players came to call this tactic simply, "The Chair," and it worked like a charm *every single time*. I looked it up, and in the games we played after using "The Chair," we never took more than three penalties, and we always won. Even better, the effect usually lasted a month or so.

This technique can certainly be applied in the real world, where one person's actions can deeply affect the entire organization, especially in the age of social media. Everyone can be doing a great job, but if one employee fires off a mean-spirited message to a client or customer, or blasts off on social media, the entire team can suffer, and everybody will be answering for the misdeed whenever someone Googles their company. Far better to make everyone understand that they're all accountable to each other *before* any of this happens. So it's your job to set up systems that link all their fates together.

Some managers tell me that in the real world you can't have employees publicly apologize to each other, or make others carry the burden of someone else's mistakes. I disagree. First, your employees are already paying for everyone else's mistakes, as I've just described, whether it's acknowledged or not. And as for apologies, I've seen great leaders and organizations handle the diciest *mea culpas* imaginable and come out better for it.

In 2001 a successful malpractice defense attorney named Rick Boothman joined the University of Michigan hospital to spearhead a radical approach to addressing medical mistakes. Instead of simply circling the wagons, going radio-silent, and hiding behind a squadron of lawyers, which most hospitals have been doing for years, Boothman advised the U-M doctors to first investigate what went wrong, then sit down with the patients and their families and explain whatever mistakes were made, answer their questions, apologize sincerely, and promise to do everything they can to remedy the situation. This radical approach — traditionally called honesty, consideration, and compassion—liberated doctors, relieved patients and their families, and slashed malpractice lawsuits *by two-thirds*.

If world-class doctors can apologize to patients face-to-face for surgeries gone wrong, your employees can apologize to their co-workers or clients for sending a nasty email. In fact, if your team is ever going to reach its potential, they must.

Critical point: whatever rules applied to my players also applied to me.

They couldn't be late. I couldn't be late—not even once.

They couldn't loaf. I couldn't loaf—ever.

They couldn't take dumb penalties. I couldn't take dumb penalties—or any penalties.

During one of our playoff games, we faced a solid team that had beaten us twice before, but we had since become the better team. Ahead 3–1 in the third period, I became convinced that the refs were picking on my guys, and I let the refs know it. The refs ignored my barking until I put my foot on the boards—a no-no—and yelled across the ice at the ref at the far end of the rink. I can't recall what I yelled, but I bet the ref can, because whatever it was, he saw fit to skate all the way across the ice to point right at me and shout, "Two minutes, bench minor!"

When a coach gets a penalty, a player on the ice has to serve his time in the penalty box. Then your players have to kill two minutes with one man down just like any other penalty. I was equal parts mortified and furious with myself. As dumb and selfish as it is to take a penalty behind the play or after the whistle, costing your players two minutes for shooting your mouth off from the bench beats them all.

Sure enough, our opponents scored, cutting our lead to 3–2 with two minutes left. I was never so anxious to see our guys put away an opponent than I was that night. God bless 'em, our players came through with two more goals, and we won, 5–3.

After the game I congratulated our guys for another great effort, and their sixteenth win — only the second Huron team ever to do that. But then I apologized profusely to them for being so selfish and promised them I would never do that again.

We had taken ten penalties in that game, but one was mine and a few were ridiculous — which is why I'd been yelling at the refs in the first place — so I didn't feel the team needed "The Chair" the next day. They had gotten the message, even if I hadn't.

So I created a new punishment just for me: running two laps around the rink's large parking lot in a cold rain. When I headed out to run before our practice, the guys watched me leave from the arena's glass-enclosed foyer. Then I pounded out probably a mile or so on the asphalt, cursing myself every step of the way. When I finished, I was shocked to see the entire team still standing at the lobby's wall of windows, watching me come back in. It obviously mattered to them that our rules mattered to me, underscoring one of the basic rules of leadership: never ask them to do anything you won't.

We witnessed the apotheosis of this approach in the middle of my third season coaching the River Rats.

Because of our strong second season, capped by our eye-opening 3–2 regional final loss to Trenton, when I started making our game schedule for our third season, I got calls for games from teams and tournaments that couldn't spell "Huron" two years earlier. These included the Michigan High School Hockey Showcase, which brought the state's best twenty-two teams together to play two games each. The idea was to make it easier for high school coaches to scout the state's best competition, and for college coaches to scout the state's best players.

We were thrilled to be invited, but when the weekend arrived months later, we knew we had our work cut out for us: we would be facing fourth-ranked Clarkston Friday night and third-ranked Muskegon Mona Shores, featuring future Detroit Red Wing star Justin Abdelkader, the very next day. Further, both games would be played at Trenton's Kennedy Arena, where we had only recently interrupted our long, sad history of getting pummeled.

Still, we were on an eight-game winning streak and had finally squeezed back into the state's top ten — at number nine — for the first time in many, many years. We were playing to win.

I was concerned, however, that our penalties had been floating upward. We had taken eight against Pioneer, ten against a Metro League foe, and then a staggering fifteen penalties by ten different players against Saline, a local high school team. To record both teams' thirty-three total penalties, the scorekeeper had to resort to a second scoresheet. Not only was this not the kind of hockey we wanted to play, we knew that if we took that many penalties against either ranked team in the Michigan High School Hockey Showcase, they'd destroy us. Heck, just one dumb penalty could cost us either game — and we'd worked too hard to get this chance to throw it away by indulging our anger.

So when we started practice the next day, our players were not surprised to see a rusty old chair at center ice. They knew the drill, they knew why, and they actually seemed to welcome it, knowing we needed to get our heads straight before the big weekend. After we finished fifteen full-speed, full-length sprints, the message had been reinforced.

When we played fourth-ranked Clarkston — a particularly well-coached team that would finish runner-up for the Division I state title — we stuck to our principles, our game plan, and our style of hockey and avoided taking any stupid, selfish penalties. Hundreds of the state's best players and coaches were watching, plus lots of hockey fans who just wanted to see a good game — and they got one. We skated with Clarkston shift for shift, and period for period, in an all-out duel. With the Rats down 1–0 with 1:09 left, Pete "Hairball" Heeringa fired one past their goalie to tie the game, 1–1 — and that's how the contest ended.

The handshaking line went slower than usual because the players felt compelled to offer more than the standard "Good game" to each other. Clarkston's coach was equally gracious: "That was great hockey!"

Even our stoic trainer, Rod Sorge, was impressed. Back in the locker room, he said, "Look at the scoresheet."

I scanned it: one goal each, shots even at 29–29 — all the signs of a great game. But I already expected to see all that, so I looked back at Sorge, unsure what point he was trying to make.

"No," Sorge said. "Look at the *penalties.*"

When I looked on the sheet under "Penalties," the scorekeeper had written in big capital letters, "NONE." Neither team had taken *a single penalty* — and it wasn't because the refs were blind, or because either team had taken the night off. Every shift was contested, every loose puck battled for, every defender played the body on every rush, and the refs were on top of it all. No, there were no penalties because every player on both teams knew how to play the game the right way, and that's exactly what they did.

"In all my years," Sorge said, "*that* was the most beautiful high school hockey game I've ever seen."

That Clarkston could play that way didn't surprise anyone watching that day. That the River Rats could play just as well surprised everyone. Everyone, that is, except us.

We followed up the next day by beating Justin Abdelkader's team, 5–4. But the highlight of the weekend for us wasn't holding the future NHL star to just one goal, but holding ourselves to zero penalties the night before in a fabulous game.

Now *that* was impressive.

When I got home that night, I wrote to our team, "If anyone doubted you belonged among the state's very best before that weekend, they certainly weren't asking any questions when you left."

- Peer pressure is a fact of life, and you're not going to get rid of it. Instead, use it to create accountability to each other among your people, which is a stronger force than accountability to the leader.

- Senpai-kohai, the Japanese mentoring system, breaks down the barriers of experience and rank by generating camaraderie and mutual obligation across generational lines.

- To leverage negative peer pressure, when one of your people crosses the line, make everyone *but* the offender suffer the consequences. When one screws up, everyone pays.

- If that guy is you, you have to pay the same penalty as your people do. Whether you pay it or don't pay it, either way they won't forget.

11

The More Power You Give, the More Power You Get

- Promote leaders based on their ability to lead, *not* their ability to do the job they have now.

- Create *layers of leadership* by delegating decision-making downstream.

- Let your people *set their own goals,* both individually and as a team, for better results.

You've probably gathered by now that I'm not too keen on pandering to your people's every whim. But just in case, let me be clear: it's worse than a waste of time — it's completely counterproductive.

I'm a big believer in setting high expectations, without apology, and working hard to help your people reach them. But that doesn't mean you can play dictator and expect them to follow either. Like I've said, the more you want from them, the more you have to give. Only fair. You want your people to come to the conclusion that working hard for you is a pretty good deal. Otherwise, they'll quit — or worse, drag the rest of your team down.

One of the most valuable things you can give your people is control. This may sound contradictory after I've just told you how essential it is to instill discipline in your troops, but the real paradox is this: the more power you have, the more you can give away — and the more power you give away, the more power you will ultimately have.

Take leadership. If you're the only leader, then it's you versus them — and they're going to win. Instead, you can create what I call *layers of leadership* — so many layers, in fact, that *most* of your employees are leading someone. I'd even take it a step farther: the only people in your organization who *don't* need to lead are your new employees — or in our case, the freshmen.

You not only want to increase the quantity of leaders in your organization, but the quality of your leaders as well.

Business leaders often make the common mistake of promoting their top salesperson to become their sales manager. This is usually a bad idea for several reasons. First, the traits needed to be an excellent salesperson often have little overlap with those needed to be an excellent leader. In fact, some of the very qualities that drive a good salesperson — aggressiveness, a degree of selfishness, and a narrow focus on numbers — can be counterproductive in leadership roles.

The same is true in other fields as well. The best surgeons are often promoted to department chairs, the best trial attorneys become managing partners, and the best engineers end up running their divisions — whether or not they want to, are ready, or have had any leadership experience or training.

Some of the greatest athletes have become some of the most unsuccessful coaches. This list includes baseball's Ted Williams, football's Bart Starr, hockey's Wayne Gretzky, and basketball's Magic Johnson, just to name a few. The reason is simple: *scoring is not the same as coaching!* And selling a lot of cars is not the same as running the entire dealership.

The contrapositive is also true: the best coaches were often mediocre athletes, at best. Phil Jackson was an average NBA player;

Bill Belichick played football at Division III Wesleyan University, never coming close to the NFL; Scotty Bowman's hockey playing career ended early with an injury; and Casey Stengel, who won nine World Series titles managing the Yankees, once said, "I had many years that I was not so successful as a ballplayer, as it is a game of skill."

Yet those four coaches won more championships than anyone else in their sport. So when it's time for you to pick your leaders, pick them not because they're your leading salesperson, attorney, surgeon, engineer, or teacher, but because they're your best *leaders*.

You might recall that, during my first lunch with our incoming captain, Mike Henry, I told him I didn't care if he scored a single goal that year. I would judge him solely on how well he led the team — nothing more.

To that end, from the very first day we gathered as a team on Henry's back deck, I referred to him only as "Captain." I would often leave the locker room after saying, "Captain — your team!" (I would treat each subsequent captain the same — and I still call all of them "Captain" to this day.) I wanted the rest of the team to know that Henry had special status, that I respected his role, that I would defer to him on many matters, and that I truly *expected* him to lead the team. When Henry needed to correct a teammate, everyone knew that he spoke for the coaches, and that we had his back.

This approach works better for everyone. I needed all the help I could get, Henry needed our support, and many of the players preferred hearing from a fellow teammate — even if it was negative, and often *especially* when it was negative — than from a coach. Yes, there is a danger that others will resent the elevation of a peer. But there's a far greater danger that if no one leads but you, your whole organization will collapse.

After Henry graduated, he helped us coach our summer team,

and he was terrific. When one player I had been pushing com-plained to Henry, "Coach hates me!" Henry told him, "Coach doesn't hate anyone. He just thinks you can do better." When Henry told me this, it made my week. More important, the player and I both ben-efited from Henry's help.

Henry would go on to captain Kent State's hockey team, and he brought two of his younger Huron teammates with him. I drove down to see them all play during Henry's senior year, and I was not surprised to see that Henry continued to be everything a captain is supposed to be.

Henry now has a wife and two kids. He's the general manager of the USA Hockey Arena in Plymouth, Michigan, home of the na-tion's top junior players, and runs the acclaimed Compuware youth hockey program, one of the country's best. He leads a staff of sixty people, with very little turnover. Henry uses a go-to phrase when he conducts interviews, delivers performance reviews, or needs to give his people a reminder: "Work hard, and have fun. To me, work hard includes supporting your teammates."

Music to his old coach's ears.

On most high school hockey teams everyone votes for the team's leading scorer to become the captain, the guy gets a "C" on his jer-sey, and that's pretty much the end of it.

Not on our team. That "C" was an honor, but also an obligation, one that came with daily duties that had to be carried out very well or we were not going to reach our potential.

That's why we picked our captains very, very carefully. We didn't even vote until all of our seniors and a few juniors had had plenty of chances to lead our stretching, workouts, relays, practices, and in-formal games, all summer and fall — a four-month tryout for a four-month season. I never meddled with the votes that followed — ev-ery player and coach got one vote each — and they always picked the right guys, every time.

Everyone understood that serving as a captain on our team was a demanding endeavor. One year our best returning player, Keith

Ferris, told me privately that if he was chosen (and he likely would have been, because he had already proven to be a great leader), he would decline the "C." He explained that his mom had a serious illness and would need his support, "and I know what a big responsibility being a captain on this team is."

I loved him for that, of course. I praised his maturity, and kept it between us. (I tell this story with his permission.)

Sure enough, Ferris received the most votes, but I kept that to myself too. Instead, I announced that two other players had been elected to serve as our co-captains. Ferris served ably as an assistant captain, led the team in scoring by a long shot, and was named the Metro League's best forward. I'm pleased to say his mother came through with flying colors too.

The opposite was also true: just because you *weren't* our leading scorer didn't mean you couldn't lead. Stevie Wasik — who told me as a sophomore, "I'd rather fill water bottles for the varsity than be captain of my travel team" — finished his junior year tied for fourteenth on our team in scoring, out of nineteen. Yet, at the start of his senior year, his teammates voted him co-captain, which shows you how much they respected Stevie and how deeply they understood how leadership really worked on our team. Not surprisingly, Stevie did a great job leading the squad.

I met with our captains every single day — could be for a half-hour or a couple minutes before they went home — just to hear how things looked from their point of view.

"Bacon would always ask about the 'mood' in the locker room," former assistant captain Bobby Chappuis recalls. "He wanted to make sure that there was always a high level of engagement and that the 'mood' was generally positive. If there were concerns, we'd address them."

Once you see your team's "mood" as your culture, the value of this is obvious.

Our seniors also had special status, and I relied on them for a host of decisions, great and small, from deciding what we were going to wear in school on game days — jerseys, sweat jackets, or green shirts and gold ties? — to handling disciplinary situations. The message was clear: these guys had paid their dues, their opinions mattered, and we were all responsible for how our team functioned, not just the coaches.

These various layers of leadership effectively broke down the polarizing "coach versus the team" dynamic by mixing things up and giving older players important roles. With layers of leadership, the younger players also had someone other than the coaches to listen to, and something to look forward to when they became seniors, captains, or both.

We enjoyed such an abundance of good leaders that we had a name for those who merely led by example: we called them "sophomores." Because all "leading by example" meant to us was that you knew your job, and you could do your job. Well, hell, everyone but a newbie should know that!

So I explained that we expected sophomores to know their jobs and to do their jobs. We expected juniors to know their jobs, to do their jobs, and to know everyone else's job too. Then we expected seniors to know their jobs, to do their jobs, to know everyone else's job, and to *help everyone do their jobs better*. That's what a team of leaders does!

It isn't enough for your veteran employees to do their jobs, give no mind to anyone else, and go home satisfied. Not even close. They've got to help others do their jobs better.

After we put our first senior class's name plaques on our locker room wall next to a new plaque that said MOST IMPROVED TEAM, we decided to do the same for all our subsequent classes too. So at the beginning of each season, I would tell our newly minted seniors that in four months we would be gluing their name plaques on our locker room wall too, with another plaque listing their team's biggest accomplishment.

Before our third season together, when I addressed the seniors-to-be in our locker room, I told them to look up at the plaques of the seniors who'd come before and their team's adjoining plaque:

2000–01: MOST IMPROVED TEAM IN
SCHOOL HISTORY (+7 WINS)
2001–02: 16-9-2. BEST SINCE 1973

Then I said: "I'm going to be here after you're gone. So this is my program, but this is *your team*. What is your team's plaque going to say when you're done? *You* will decide what we write at the end of the year, not me. So lead your team like you mean it."

This approach worked so well that after our first year together, when I had taught all of them just about everything that I expected of them, I didn't have to tell the next team much at all. By our second year, only the freshmen were new, so the seniors could teach them – which they did, eagerly, because they believed in our principles and wanted *their* team to succeed. When I saw a freshman doing something stupid or inappropriate, which happened only several times a day, I would look around and ask, with an exaggerated sigh, "Is there a senior here who could help young Mr. Jacobs?"

And that's how layers of leadership work. The point is this: you already have the titles and honors to identify your next layers of leaders – and if you don't, or don't have enough, you need to create more, based on any criteria you see fit, including seniority or a vote of their peers. Then transform those titles into meaningful leadership roles to help everyone improve the daily functioning of your organization and take ownership of their team.

So I say, take it a step farther: Yes, titles and name plaques are nice. But don't just give them a title and a name plaque. Give them *responsibility*, and let them lead.

For our third season, I set up a diabolical schedule, with seventeen of our twenty-six games against teams in the top ten of the state's three divisions. (In Michigan high school hockey, a top-ranked Division III team can usually beat all but a few Division I teams.) We started the season by tying a good Metro League team 4–4, then lost to Trenton, 5–4, with one of our best players out of the lineup. Painful, but at least we proved our 3–2 playoff loss to Trenton wasn't a fluke. We now felt we could play shift-for-shift with them.

We soon got it going, winning a tough Thanksgiving tournament and knocking off two more teams before facing archrival Pioneer in front of a full house on a Wednesday night. My Culver mentor Al Clark and his wife Blair took two days off from coaching and teaching to make the eight-hour round trip to see the game. Pretty much everyone I knew in town would be in the stands that night. I didn't get any other work done that week.

"I remember how badly I wanted to beat Pioneer," Pete "Hairball" Heeringa, recalls. "It always felt like a biblical reckoning, like the story of the haves versus the have-nots. They *needed* to be beaten."

I felt the same way. We *could* have beaten them our first year, before the tennis balls flew. We *should* have beaten them our second year, when we completely outplayed them in both games before losing the first one, 4–3, and tying the second one, 4–4.

"If you go too long without beating your rival," I told the *Ann Arbor News*, "it becomes more than a game and you feel like you're fighting history."

Our third year, with the Clarks in the stands, we knew we needed to stop this streak from snowballing one game longer — and our guys played like it, taking command from the start and putting the Pioneers away, 4–2. In the final minutes, the Pioneers were so befuddled by our defensive schemes that they barely even tried to take the puck out of their own end, knowing we were just going to stop them and throw the puck back into their zone and make them try again.

"We want this program to be about more than wins and losses," I told the newspaper reporter afterward, "but this is our biggest win in a long time."

Steve Sheldon, the parent who had worked with our trainer Rod Sorge on the search committee to persuade the others to vote for me, told Sorge, "My work here is done."

When I saw my parents in the lobby after the game, my father shook my hand, looked me in the eye, but was too choked up to speak. When Pete Uher's parents congratulated us, Pete blurted out that I knew some Czech, their native language. Pete laughed because he knew I could say only one phrase, "jsem v prdeli," which loosely translates, "I'm fucked." Pete's father Ctirad pulled me aside so I could whisper my only Czech words. He laughed and said, "Not tonight you are not!"

We gathered for a postgame celebration at a nearby sports bar, with coaches, parents, friends, and the Clarks in attendance. It was something to savor.

The Rats kept the fire burning through fourteen games — more than half our season — without a single loss, setting another school record. The streak covered almost all of December and January — the opposite of our ten-game losing streak two years earlier. More deliciously, we were getting revenge on all the teams that had trounced us the past few years, night after night.

"In just four years," recalls Bobby Chappuis, a senior that year, "we went from losing every game as a freshman to stepping onto the ice with the attitude that our opponent should be afraid of *us*. All the little things — the practice agendas, the Monday study halls, the X's and O's game plans — had added up and we were able to execute well. We'd seen the videotape, we *knew* the game plan, and we *believed* in the game plan."

Our guys were not cocky, flashy, or arrogant. They always celebrated their goals as a team, with no showboating. But their confidence ran deep, rooted in three years of intense effort and sacrifice, and it occasionally manifested itself as well-earned swagger.

"We knew who we were, and we knew that we had put in the work to beat anyone we came across," says Stevie Wasik, now a vice president at Insight Global. "That kind of confidence changes you, and you start seeking that feeling in other areas of your life."

I occasionally enjoyed walking into our locker room before a game and telling our guys, "Our opponents just made a big mistake."

"What'd they do?" someone would ask.

"They got off the bus," I'd say. "They're going to regret that."

. . .

On January 30, the fourth-ranked River Rats visited top-ranked Trenton. We trailed 4–3 in the third period before Trenton pulled away for a 6–3 victory. Three days later against Pioneer we couldn't convert any of our nine power play opportunities and lost 3–0.

The next day we turned in our only bad practice of the season, and now I was getting paranoid that we'd just started a losing streak. So I decided we needed to mix things up. But how?

Whenever someone came up to me during one of our workouts – our athletic director, say, or a teacher, or a parent – I would tell our seniors, "You guys know what to do," then let them take over the workout while I talked to our visitor. As soon as our guest departed I'd tell our guys how much that impressed me. You could see how proud that made them feel.

Well, that gave me an idea. The night before our next game – against a downriver team that was definitely good enough to beat us and would soon be admitted to the Metro League – I called our captain, Chris Fragner, and told him that he and his fellow seniors would be coaching the team for that game. Not leading, but *coaching*.

"What do you mean?" Fragner asked.

"From the time you get to the locker room to the time you talk to the *Ann Arbor News* reporter after the game, you and your classmates will be doing everything the coaches do: decide who starts, who plays, when to change lines, what to say – you name it."

"Wow – really?" Fragner asked. "Okay!"

"Don't worry," I said. "I wouldn't ask you to do this if you couldn't handle it – and I know you can handle it. If you have any questions, the coaches will be there in the locker room and on the bench with you, but we'll only speak when spoken to."

So Fragner told his buddies, and word quickly spread. By the time everyone got to the rink, they already knew they would be in charge that night, from filling out the lineup to giving a pregame speech and doing the chalk-talks between periods. They were excited and a little nervous, but they dived right in, they did it all, and they enjoyed it. They had a few laughs, but they took it seriously, as I knew they would. The last thing they wanted was to lose three straight games, which was a real possibility.

Not to worry. They coached and played a great game, blowing out a solid team, 6–0.

The *Ann Arbor News* headline read, "Seniors Carry Huron to Victory: Bacon's Team Sizzles after Players Take over Coaching Responsibilities." The reporter wrote, "If John Bacon keeps making such smart coaching decisions, he might be out of a job."

Hey, that was the idea!

Fragner told the reporter, "[Bacon] tries to give the players a lot of say in things all year. He didn't think this would be a big deal."

"It's funny what can happen when you relax," I told the paper. "It's a special group of guys that can run the whole show. It worked out great, and I'm not surprised."

The victory not only started us on another winning streak, it showed the seniors – and everyone else too – just what they could do.

You can do this too: tell your people to take over *your* job for one day. They'll learn what it takes to lead, and you'll learn about them. Everybody wins.

Most organizations just post the group's goals on a PowerPoint slide – and that's it. The employees usually have no input whatsoever, they've never seen those goals before, and they likely will never see them again. Needless to say, those goals will have no impact on their performance or behavior – and they will never be reached.

In contrast, every year we picked ten team goals. I laid down only the first two: highest team grade point average in the state and lowest penalty minutes in the league. To pick our next eight goals, the captains and seniors would run the meeting, brainstorming with the entire team using a whiteboard. I'd give the seniors a cou-

ple dozen ideas they could draw on, but they always expanded, edited, and altered the list to make it their own. *That's exactly what I
wanted them to do.*

They always came up with good goals too. Not just to beat our
archrival, Pioneer, and later Trenton, but, at first, to win ten games,
then fifteen. To win our Metro League division, then the entire
league. To score a hundred goals and give up fewer than fifty. To win
"revenge" games against a list of teams that had beaten us the year
before. And to claim the mythical "County Crown," something we
made up, that entailed beating the local small-town teams outside
of our league—a nice way to stay hungry for those games in which
we otherwise wouldn't be playing for much. Our second year the
team even set the goal of "Shut out Dexter on Senior Night"—then
did it, 6–0, with Scooter scoring the last goal with three seconds left.

And don't worry about your people setting the bar too low.
I quickly discovered that *they never will*. The real danger is that
they'll set it too high. But by our third year, *nothing* was too high,
including their tenth goal: "STATE CHAMPIONS!"

Two years earlier—on Monday, June 26, 2000, at our very first
workout—when I told them we would soon be competing for a state
title, they understandably thought I was nuts. Two years later, *they*
were saying that. After our previous team had almost beaten Trenton in the regional final, no one in the state thought they were nuts.

When they finished setting their goals, you could see how proud
they were of what they'd done and how excited they were to get going. I took their list, made a few copies, laminated them, and posted
them in highly visible spots around the locker room.

They did such a good job with it that we always had at least a few
of our ten goals at stake every time we played, which is a wonderful
thing. At the start of each practice, I'd remind them which of their
goals were on the line that week. After each game we would take a
pen and update the goals we had achieved, advanced, or failed to
reach.

I admit I really don't know how much it mattered *what* goals
they picked, so long as their goals were ambitious, achievable,

and *came from them*. Everyone is more motivated to achieve their own goals than someone else's — *so let 'em!* And if they achieve the goals they picked, they'll probably accomplish a lot of the ones you wanted to check off too.

I also asked the players to spend a day or two thinking about five individual goals they wanted to achieve that year. I would then meet with each of them in the coaches' room to discuss their goals, and we'd add their list to a laminated card, with the ten team goals on the front and the five individual goals on the back. (I kept a copy of each for myself, as a point of discussion whenever I met individually with the players.)

The same principles applied: if they set their own goals, they were more motivated to achieve them. If we wrote the goals down and they discussed them with me, they were more accountable. But unlike our team goals, we kept their personal goals private so they would feel safe dreaming big.

Picking their team goals came with a catch. On the rare day that we weren't putting all we had into our workout, practice, or game, I could tell them to pull out their goal cards from their wallets and ask them to read their team goals. After they finished, I would say, "Now, correct me if I'm wrong, but those are all *your* goals, correct? You guys came up with those yourselves, you debated what to keep, and the ones you finally picked were all *your* ideas, right?"

When they nodded, I'd say, "Well, I've got news for you. What I just saw out there ain't gonna cut it. You say those are your goals, but if you're not willing to work to achieve them, then you're not serious. You're just talking a good game, but not backing it up. Now, that's not what I think of you. I've been around you guys a lot, and you really have been the hardest-working high school hockey team in the state. But not today.

"So make up your mind. If those are your goals, do you mean it or not? If you want our help, we'll give you all you need. But you have to decide for yourselves if you really want to work to achieve them." Then I'd say, "Captains, seniors — your room," and walk out.

Then the leaders would take over, and I guarantee you: when

they went back on the ice they looked like a different team, motivated by *their* goals.

That doesn't mean we achieved all our goals. In fact, we never did — although I thought that was a good sign too. If we hit all ten every year, we were setting the bar too low. If we went zero-for-ten, we either set the bar too high, didn't work hard enough, or both. I felt that achieving six to eight goals was the sweet spot, and that's what we usually hit.

I can think of no better example of the power of goal-setting than the story of Rob DeMuro.

In my first summer, Rob DeMuro (pronounced De-Meer-O, as in "hero"), then a freshman, attended every off-ice session and demonstrated good skills on the ice. But the five-foot-eight forward weighed 275 pounds and just couldn't keep up. So I cut him.

The next year he did it all again, but he still weighed 275. So I cut him.

Our third year, DeMuro's junior season, he showed up to all our summer workouts once more, which earned him the respect of the coaches and players. He played varsity football that fall, which prevented him from making our normal tryout week, so it would have been very easy for him to give up on the idea of trying out a third time.

But he screwed up his courage and asked me if he could try out after the football season finished. I agreed to give him a five-day tryout, during our practices. (We did this for anyone whose fall season ran long.) But that meant Rob would be the only guy trying out amid a squad of serious players who had already made a highly competitive team. He was quite nervous, which is understandable, but the guys truly admired him for coming out again, and their opinions mattered too.

On Friday, after the fourth of his five tryout days, I asked him whether he was serious about making the team. DeMuro recalls having the clear impression that I was "not convinced, because I hadn't made any progress with my weight."

He was right: he had talent, but he still weighed 275, so I was about to cut him a third time when his tryout ended on Monday. But after I'd confronted DeMuro he went home that weekend and talked to his dad, who told Rob he needed to prove to me that he was committed to getting in shape. That's when Rob decided to write down his plan.

Right before his last tryout that Monday, he had the guts to knock on the coaches' room door. I was going over something with an assistant, so I barked, "Yeah?" without looking up.

DeMuro walked in, "nervous as hell," he remembers, and handed me a typed sheet.

"What's this?" I asked.

"It's my plan to get in shape," he said, his voice quivering.

It was a pretty conventional list, except for point number six: "Follow the Five Ps."

"Okay, I'll bite," I said, turning to him. "What the hell are the five Ps?"

He straightened up and announced, with complete earnestness, "Perfect Preparation Prevents Piss-poor Performance, Coach."

I had to turn away, struggling not to laugh out loud. I thought, *Kid, you just made the damn team.* But I didn't tell him that. Instead, I said, "Thank you, Mr. DeMuro. We'll see you on the ice."

After his last tryout that day, he knocked on the coaches' open door again. He had every reason to believe he was about to get cut for a third straight year. So when I stood up, extended my hand, and said, "Congratulations, Mr. DeMuro, you just made the Huron hockey team," he was shocked.

I believed in him, but that didn't count for much. More important, I believed *he* would finally start believing in *himself.* That's when real progress starts.

I didn't want DeMuro, already a junior, to spend the season filling water bottles. I wanted him to lose some weight, get in a game, and maybe change his life. So I challenged him: once he lost twenty pounds, he would dress for the next game. I thought it might take him all season to do it, if he ever did—but I never told him that, of course.

Since it was a Monday, we walked down the hall to a big room where we conducted our weekly two-hour study table, with pizza brought in. "Gentlemen," I said, "I have an announcement: Rob De-Muro has just made the Huron hockey team!"

They sent up a big cheer. They loved him.

"See?" Keith Ferris, one of our stars, told him. "You keep working hard and good things happen." I liked hearing that. They felt the program was a fair meritocracy.

"I was thrilled," DeMuro recalls, "and remember thinking that I needed to get into the lineup as soon as possible."

We worked with our trainer, Rod Sorge, who supervised De-Muro. When you need to lose that much weight, the main thing is to keep hydrating.

"Looking back, what I was doing they now call intermittent fasting," DeMuro says. He replaced his big bowl of cereal with an orange, his unhealthy snacks with fruit, and Gatorade with water, largely skipped lunch, and then ate a full dinner, with his mom swapping pasta for chicken or fish.

"At first it was tough," DeMuro recalls, "but then your body learns that you don't need food all the time and I got used to it. Losing weight had its challenges, but when you're working out and skating four times a week with a group of people all supporting you, it's not as hard. There was no way I could let those people down."

I bought a digital scale just for DeMuro, and he weighed in every Friday in front of the team. (Even personal goals are often best achieved by making them public.) Then we marked his weight on the board to provide encouragement and accountability.

The first time DeMuro stepped on the scale, "it was scary," he recalls, and it got scarier when it flashed ERROR-ERROR-ERROR. "I thought, *Well that's not good. It won't even register my weight!*"

But when he stepped on it again, it said he'd already lost five pounds – a good start. "That gave me the momentum to keep going, and the confidence that it could be done."

The first month DeMuro kept losing five pounds a week, which he knew would put him very close to breaking the twenty-pound mark right before our game against Pioneer.

"That was going to be the first big game of the year," he recalls. "The stadium would be packed, and there was no way I wanted to be stuck in the stands for that."

Because I had been preoccupied with preparing for Pioneer, I had forgotten DeMuro was getting that close. So the day before the big game, when a few players rushed into the coaches' room to tell me, "Coach! You gotta come out here!" I had no idea what they were so excited about.

"What is it?" I said, staring at our lineup sheet.

"You just gotta come out here!"

"Okay," I said, dropping my work. "Must be important."

With the whole team watching, Rob DeMuro stepped on that scale, and I swear to God it flashed "254.5," exactly 20.5 pounds less than his weight when we made our deal.

He'd done it! Rob's teammates cheered, then ran around collecting all his gear for his first game – team helmet, gloves, game socks.

"Getting the new gloves and pants and picking out my number was really exciting," DeMuro recalls. "Plus knowing I would be in the lineup, it was incredible."

When he went home that night, he walked through the door with his team gloves on to show his mom. "I'm dressing!"

The next night, when DeMuro was sitting on the bench with his teammates to start the game, I saw a bunch of girls pressing handmade signs against the glass with slogans like HEY DEMURO! YOU'RE MY HERO! and chanting his name.

I tapped his helmet. "Look at this! I played three years for Huron, and you haven't even played your *first shift* yet and you already have a freakin' fan club!"

You already know we beat the archrival Pioneers that night, 4–2, resulting in rowdy celebrations in the stands, on the ice, and in our locker room. On that basis you'd have to conclude that having De-Muro in the lineup didn't hurt us and probably helped us stay relaxed and motivated at the same time.

"It's something I'll never forget," DeMuro says today, almost two decades later.

Under Sorge's supervision, DeMuro dropped five pounds every two weeks. By midseason he was getting regular playing time and making the most of it.

With a month left in our third season together, we took our 13-3-3 record and number-five state ranking on a four-hour charter bus ride to Culver, Indiana, for a two-game series against the Culver "B" team, which would have been good enough to compete for a state title in Michigan. I scheduled Culver only after I felt we'd be good enough to play in front of my mentor, Al Clark, who was still coaching Culver's "A" team, and not embarrass ourselves.

If playing at Trenton was intimidating, playing at Culver was downright terrifying, starting with their trophy cases — plural. Their players were scarily similar to Trenton's: they were all so good that I couldn't tell their first line from their fourth line. I turned to assistant coach Pete Uher, who had played his last year of high school hockey at Culver, and confessed, "These guys could beat us by ten."

Instead, our guys did everything exactly right and followed our game plan to a tee. Incredibly, they blew out Culver, 9–2. A bigger surprise: Rob DeMuro scored his first goal, and his second, and his *third* — a hat trick! — to be the leading scorer that night.

After the game, I joined Clark at Papa's Restaurant for burgers, beers, and a lot of hockey talk — as good as it gets. The next day we finished the sweep, 7–4, to send us on a very happy four-hour bus trip home, cruising past snow-covered fields on a sunny afternoon.

"This weekend," I wrote them, "was exactly what I dreamed of, on and off the ice, when I became the head coach. You impressed everyone."

It didn't take long for word to get out about our secret weapon. After the *Ann Arbor News* and Detroit's Channel 4 did feature stories on DeMuro, his teammates gave him a new nickname: "The Celebrity."

When the season ended, I told DeMuro that if he got below 200 pounds before our last summer workout at Michigan Stadium, I would carry *him* up the stadium stairs. Well, I'll be damned, the kid did it again, and it wasn't even close: he came in at 195 pounds. I kept my word and hauled him up the steps of Michigan Stadium — walking that time, not running — and we have the pictures to prove it.

The next year DeMuro moved up to the second line, scoring a remarkable twenty-five points in twenty-six games, second on the team behind only the Metro League's best forward, our own Keith Ferris. Against undefeated, second-ranked Pioneer, DeMuro scored our first goal in a 3–2 victory. He earned All-State honorable mention, his grades jumped from a C-average to a B-average, and he finished the year at 185 pounds — a full ninety pounds less than he weighed during tryouts as a junior. He earned a bachelor's degree at Western Michigan in business, with a double major in accountancy and finance, and now works as a sales operations lead for Thomson Reuters on a three-person team that supports 1,200 salespeople in three offices.

Just shows you what a little goal-setting can do.

- **The more power you have, the more you can give away — which in turn will only give you more power.**

- **If it's you versus them, you'll lose. To end that tug-of-war you need to create layers of leadership, starting with your assistants, division heads, veteran employees, and the like. Doing this benefits everyone and will also keep you from burning out.**

- **Pick your leaders not on metrics like their sales figures, but solely on their ability to *lead*. Leaders must know their jobs, know how to do their jobs, know everyone else's jobs, and *help them all do their jobs better!***

- Let your leaders make as many decisions as possible — including discipline and personnel issues — to make them responsible for how the entire team performs. This also lets the rest of your people know they are accountable to everyone, not just you.

- Let your team determine their goals, then write them down, make them public, and make sure everyone is accountable for achieving them. After all, these are *their* goals! The same holds true with individual goals: make them measurable, ambitious, achievable, and, when appropriate, public, with rewards for achieving them.

12

All Credit Goes to Your People — Not You

- If your team fails, you have to take full responsibility — but you're also allowed to fix it.

- If you're a leader, you will be criticized. It's unavoidable, so take criticism as a compliment.

- If your team succeeds, you can't take credit, because they did it, not you. The reward of a job well done is to have done it.

Any leader will face a lot of tough times, but the toughest might be those minutes immediately after suffering a heartbreaking setback. The second trickiest might be the minutes following a big success — and no, I'm not kidding, because success presents almost as many potential potholes as failure.

In business, this happens all the time: you get bad news or great news right in the middle of a workday, surrounded by your people. Fair or not, what you say next will have a profound effect on how they respond to the news — and to you.

A flashback: Senior Night of our first season, when goalie Steve

Beltran played the game of his life to pull off an upset over a league rival for our record seventh win. I walked off the ice and jammed both fists into the air, a spontaneous gesture of relief, triumph, and pride. Whenever I see that picture, I understand how I felt at that moment, but I still wince. I believe it marked the only time I did anything like that after our team won—and for good reason: it wasn't my place.

Let me explain. When Herb Brooks's 1980 Olympic hockey team beat the Soviets in the greatest upset in the history of sports, it marked the culmination of his own incredible two-decade journey.

I wrote my first story about Brooks and the 1980 US Olympic hockey team for the *Detroit News* in 1996, and I followed up with several more stories over the years until he subsequently agreed to write a book with me in the spring of 2003, a couple of months after my third season coaching Huron. I flew to Minnesota that May so that Herb and I could sit down for a long interview—the first of many, we assumed.

In that discussion, Brooks told me a few things he'd never said publicly before. When he played college hockey at Minnesota, his primary goal was to make the US Olympic team, and he did so in 1960. Or so he thought. He even stood for the team photo just days before the Squaw Valley Olympics. But when Harvard's star player, Bill Cleary, and his brother Bob decided at the last minute that they both wanted to play in the Olympics, the head coach gave Bob Cleary Herb's spot. They also gave Cleary Herb's body: in the team photo, they carved out Herb's head and replaced it with Bob's. That 1960 team won the first Olympic gold medal for the United States in ice hockey, while Herb watched the game with his father back home in St. Paul on a little black-and-white TV.

While the gold medals were being draped around his teammates' necks, Herb's dad said, "Looks like they cut the right guy."

Others have reported that remark, but not what Herb's father said next: "You had a dream. If you're willing to work for your dream and sacrifice for your dream, don't let anyone, even me, talk you out of it."

Herb took the advice. After that painful setback, he launched his career as an insurance salesman and started a family with his wife Patti, but he continued to play at the highest level of US amateur hockey. His commitment paid off when he captained the US Olympic teams in 1964 and 1968, though neither team won any medals.

In 1972, when Brooks became head coach at his alma mater, the University of Minnesota, the Gophers were dead last with seven wins against twenty-seven losses. But Herb's goal wasn't merely to turn the Gophers around, or to win the school's first NCAA title (which they would do in 1974, and again in 1976 and 1979). No, he told me, "my goal was to become the head coach of the 1980 Olympic hockey team and beat the Soviets."

Since the Soviets had just shocked the world that fall by pushing Team Canada, filled with NHL All-Stars, to the final minute of their series, Herb's dream was crazy. When I pointed this out, Herb asked me, "What's your favorite movie?"

"*Casablanca*," I answered. "What's yours?"

"You're not going to believe this," he said, grinning. "*Willy Wonka and the Chocolate Factory.*"

I looked up from my keyboard. "You've got to be kidding me."

"Nope," he said. "Here's why: it's because we've forgotten how to dream."

This got to me — as I'm sure he knew it would. I followed up. "Would you ever have been so driven to win the gold medal in 1980 if you hadn't been the last man cut in 1960 — and they hadn't won the gold without you?"

"You know, no one's ever asked me that," he said, which surprised me. "No. No, I wouldn't have. If I'd been on the 1960 team, I would've packed my gold medal away and built my insurance practice and gotten on with my life."

That lasting wound explained Herb's twenty-year quest to fulfill his dream — to win the Olympic gold medal he had been denied — and makes the climax all the more amazing. In 1980, when the American college kids beat the Soviets, perhaps the greatest hockey team ever assembled, the video shows Brooks looking up at the scoreboard to make sure it's true, thrusting his fists in the air, then watching his players celebrate, beaming at them with a deep pride, respect, and affection.

And that's the last you see of Herb Brooks. He didn't jump on the ice, or shake the Soviets' hands, or hug his players. He quietly walked underneath the stands, slipped into an unused locker room, and cried — unseen.

Two days later, when the US team beat Finland to secure the gold medal, same thing: no Brooks after the final horn, or on the podium, or on the little stand where US captain Mike Eruzione famously waved all his teammates up to join him.

Why?

"They did all the work," Herb told me, "so they get all the credit."

And there's your lesson, from the architect of the greatest upset in the history of sports. If he could walk away from that most famous of celebrations, we can walk away from ours.

When I took over the winless Huron hockey team, the potential dangers of taking credit for great triumphs did not strike me as my most immediate concern. But it wasn't long before we started winning some games, and I realized handling success was something I had to think about. After Beltran's Senior Night triumph and my embarrassing display, the Rats won two summer league trophies, a school-record thirty-three high school games in two seasons, and three Thanksgiving tournaments, among other titles.

When your team wins a trophy, the PA announcer calls for the head coach to come accept it. And this is when I thought of Herb, jammed my hands into my pockets, and nodded for our captain to go get *his* trophy and to skate it around the rink with his teammates, while I walked off to the locker room. After a while, our players learned the drill: they did the work, they got the trophy, they got to celebrate.

If a reporter talked to me on the way back to our locker room, I always gave all credit to the players, which only makes sense. When I joined the players in the locker room to recap the game, I praised the players as a team, then individually when we called up that night's big contributors to tear off the sheets. The players quickly figured out that none of their coaches would ever take credit for their success.

I'm not arguing for false modesty, but for accountability. Like Herb said: they do the work, they get the credit. But accountability is a two-sided coin.

Because of our deal, I could remind the team once or twice a year, after an uncharacteristically sluggish period, "Hey, you guys get all the credit when we win, and you should. After all, you do all the work. But that's also why, privately, you'll be getting the blame tonight if you don't pick it up. This is on you. You're responsible for whatever happens next. So what's it going to be? Seniors, your room."

Then I'd walk out. What do you think happened next?

Never failed. They'd play great, win the game — and yes, get the credit.

But hey, they'd earned it.

Now, *why* can't you take credit for your team's success?

Let me answer with an example. Our first team had lost Huron's top three goal-scorers from the previous team to graduation, and our players still doubled our total goals scored from 33 to 66, then almost doubled it again the next year to 120. They did this while cutting our goals-against from 145 to 63 — or a 57 percent reduction. Pretty dramatic swings. Yet I didn't score any more goals as a coach than I had as a player. (Zero, just to remind you.) I also didn't throw a single body check, I didn't block a single shot, and I didn't make a single save. So quite obviously, all those goals were scored and saved by the guys in uniform, *not* by their coaches.

This is why I often told my players: "On game nights, your coaches wear shoes. We can't fight for loose pucks or make any hits or passes or shots or goals. *You* are going to be the only ones who can do all those things. So when you come through, all credit goes to you guys wearing skates."

Or as New York Yankees manager Casey Stengel said, "Managing is getting paid for home runs someone else hits."

Not only did our players do all those things, but they did them all voluntarily. Yes, the coaches provided principles and practices and tried to motivate our players a hundred different ways, but ultimately leaders really can't make anyone do anything.

The dean of Michigan's Ross School of Business, Scott DeRue, once explained to me, "When you're the dean, you have to lead as if you have no power — because you have no power." DeRue is a highly successful dean not *in spite of* this fact, but because he understands it — and leads accordingly.

When you're the head coach, the teacher, or the boss, you're the conductor of the orchestra. You're the one standing on the podium in your tuxedo tails, you have the baton, and you have your back to the audience. That's all pretty cool, but here's the punch line: *the baton makes no sound.* When you raise it to start the song, you better hope like hell the people in front of you decide to play.

If we can't make anyone do anything, we *can* help them *want* to do something. The rest is up to them — just like you'd want it to be. But that's why, when they come through, they get the credit for it.

I couldn't make our players run faster than they ever had before. Only they could do that — and they did. I didn't figure out that the faster runners could cut our team's relay time by waiting for the slower runners. They did that too. I couldn't make them block shots, pass, or shoot. I couldn't make the seniors take the freshmen out to lunch. I couldn't make the players embrace all the new things we were trying to do — or go so far beyond what I'd asked.

I could only hope to make them *want* to do it — which isn't saying much. That's why I could only watch in admiration as they greatly exceeded my expectations.

I believe in individual free will. It was always up to the them, and the proof was obvious: I don't think another high school hockey team has ever done what they did.

Captain Mike Henry, Elmo Eldredge, and Steve Beltran could all have bailed after I told them I expected more. Scooter McConnell could have given up after going fifty games without scoring a goal. Rob DeMuro didn't have to try out three times, and no one could make him lose ninety pounds but him.

Mark Moran, a top defenseman who'd played with Frags and Hairball since they were little kids, decided to transfer from Pioneer to play for us his junior year. That required his sitting out two-thirds of our season, an incredible sacrifice. I couldn't compel him to do that, nor could I make him an exemplary "reserve player" for those three months, which he spent filling water bottles and doing stats as well as any taxi player. The next year he earned First Team All-State. That was all him.

Frags and Hairball chose to leave their high-profile travel hockey program to join us, on our terms — no star treatment. A few other superb travel team players going to our school decided Huron hockey wasn't for them. Fair enough — but it just makes me that much more impressed by the decision that those two made.

We could only give our players the opportunities to make these choices. The rest was up to them. They made their decisions, they handled the pressure, they achieved the success, they won the trophies. It was all *theirs.*

If that's not enough, here's another reason you shouldn't take credit for your people's success: they don't like it. If you take credit for their success, they will never work as hard for you again.

And don't worry: if you're the leader of a successful team, you will *always* get more credit than you deserve. Even if you don't, Ralph Waldo Emerson got it right when he said, "The reward of a job well done is to have done it."

On the flip side, guess who gets the blame when your team fails? Why, you do of course — *all of it.* And rightly so, because you either picked the wrong people, trained them poorly, let them develop bad habits, or otherwise led your team to defeat. You own it — and you can't say anything else publicly.

Now, privately, you have the power to analyze what led to that setback, figure out how to fix it, and make the necessary changes, however painful. But that's what Monday is for. It's best not to make everything worse by blaming someone else first.

When Mack Brown coached the University of Texas football team, he told me how he learned this lesson after a tough loss. In the press conference, Brown mentioned that his players hadn't performed up to his expectations. When he got home that evening, his mentor, the Longhorns' legendary former coach Darrell Royal, called him up.

"Coach, can I give you a little advice?"

"Sure."

"After a game, the people of Texas want to hear one of only two things from their head coach: if you won, they want you to brag on your players; and if you lost, they want to hear you say, 'It was my fault,' because they already think that anyway."

Before D-Day, General Dwight Eisenhower wrote to the 160,000 troops about to land on the beaches of Normandy: "I have full confidence in your courage, devotion to duty, and skill in battle."

But Eisenhower also wrote another letter in case the mission failed: "My decision to attack at this time and place was based upon the best information available. The troops, the air, and the Navy did all that bravery and devotion to duty could do. If any blame or fault attaches to the attempt, it is mine alone."

And that is what a real leader sounds like.

A related point: if you are a leader, you will take some shots — guaranteed.

During my four years coaching the Rats the feedback I got from our players and parents was overwhelmingly positive, including frequent praise, amazingly thoughtful and generous gifts, and tons of help. I consider all the players and almost all the parents good friends to this day. But I still received two surprisingly nasty, personal emails from two mothers who felt their sons should be getting more playing time. I can't say those emails felt good — I can still remember them years later — but I've heard enough horror stories from teachers, coaches, and other leaders to know that on the grand scale, I was quite lucky.

Just remember: if you're a leader, criticism comes with the territory. Plumbers get wet. Beekeepers get stung. And leaders get criticized.

During Chris Fragner's senior year, I thought he was the best player in the state, and his friend Pete Heeringa was an inch behind. I sent out letters with their statistics to every head coach in the state to encourage them to vote both players for First Team All-State, and Fragner for Mr. Hockey, awarded to the state's best player.

The joke went that only one man could keep Fragner from winning that top award — and that man was me, his coach. Whenever we had a decent third-period lead, I pulled our stars to give the third- and fourth-line players more ice time. I probably cost Frags and Hairball ten goals each, and Fragner the Mr. Hockey title, which he lost in an extremely close vote. Neither player ever complained. As we told all the players and parents at the outset of each season, nobody was going to get everything they wanted — but everyone would get what they needed.

Fragner had a target on his back whenever he took the ice. Every coach told their players to key on him all game long. As a result, Frags probably took more hacks and whacks than anyone in the state. One night he came to the bench grumbling about all the crap he was taking, and I sympathized.

"You're right, Captain. They're hacking and whacking you, and the refs are missing most of it. I'm on the refs as much as I can be without getting a penalty myself. It ain't fair. But I actually know how you can end it forever."

"Really?!" he said hopefully, looking over his shoulder.

"Yeah," I said. "I can make it so you never get hacked and whacked again!"

"How's that?!"

"You can suck like I did. If you don't have the puck — or even better, if you're on the bench — no one will ever bother you."

That's the point: if you have the puck and you're the best player in the state, you're going to get whacked. Likewise, if you're a leader, you're going to get criticized.

When you do get criticized, take the advice of my friend Steve Edwards, who's served as interim CEO of WBEZ–Chicago Public Radio and still leads the content team. He told me there are two mistakes you can make with criticism: listen to none of it, or listen to all of it. If you listen to none of it, you risk missing something important. If you listen to all of it, you won't be able to sleep. The trick is learning what to take seriously and what to ignore, and you learn that by developing better judgment and thicker skin.

Three games after the triumphant weekend sweeping Culver's B-team, we were ranked fifth in the state. For our first playoff game we'd face the state's ninth-ranked team. If we won that game, we'd face the seventh-ranked team, then the third-ranked team, followed by the state's first-ranked team. Our draw was easily the toughest in the state — and even winning all those games would only get us to the final four, where we'd be certain to face two more great teams. But as one of our hockey parents said, "You are a team of destiny."

That's how we felt — and our potential opponents must have agreed, because they all sent coaches to scout us. Even the local paper must've seen it that way. When we won our first playoff game, 5–2, the *Ann Arbor News* ran the story with a big headline, "Huron Begins Its March."

We had a 17-3-5 record, already Huron's best, but we didn't stop to congratulate ourselves. We were gunning for nothing less than a state title.

We had to play our second playoff game without our second-line center, who had injured his wrist on Senior Night. Early in the game we lost our second right winger to a concussion. Nonetheless, we still controlled play, outshooting the seventh-ranked team, 32–16. But their goalie was hot that night, forcing us to come from behind 2–0, and then 3–2 before we tied the game at 3–3 in the third period to force overtime.

We still had little doubt we were going to win the game and advance to the next round — but in overtime their leading scorer stole the puck from one of our best players, dashed to our net, and shot a beautiful backhand over our goalie's shoulder.

4–3. Game over.

Season over.

Dreams dashed.

The player who'd lost the puck started banging his head against the glass in agony. But I noticed that our guys immediately surrounded him in a group hug. They didn't have to be told to support their teammate.

If we had won, we would have played the third-ranked Brighton Bulldogs, a team we respected tremendously. They would go on to win five state titles. Their coach, Paul Moggach, had been scouting us. Years later, he still remembered our game because it was so surprising.

"I wasn't even taking notes on the other guys, because we all figured you were going to win," he said. "You guys did everything *but* win. Complete domination."

Seventeen years later, the coach of the team that upset us told a mutual friend, "We had no business winning that game." Well, he was right about that. But that's hockey.

It was the toughest loss I've ever suffered, and I'm sure it was for our players too. In the *Ann Arbor News* story, titled, "Huron Heartbroken," I said, "It's heartbreaking because they put their whole hearts in it. They played a fantastic game. They clearly played well enough to win."

Assistant coach Pete Uher remembers, "The expectation of success makes failure that much more painful. We should have beat them, and if we played them ten times, we'd win nine. But . . ."

But . . . there was no getting it back. No do-overs. No appeals. No second chances.

In our locker room, our guys were virtually catatonic. They already knew how I felt about them, but I needed to say it again. "You proved your mettle by fighting back to tie the game *twice*. The game didn't end the way we wanted it to, but the best team doesn't always win. More important, to me, you exemplified the two principles of Huron hockey: you worked hard, and you supported your teammates instinctively, without being told, the second the game ended."

I told them how proud I was of them — not just for another great effort but for a great season, and a great three years. They had covered more ground than any team in the country, and they knew it.

But no words could take the sting out. Our locker room was silent for a full fifteen minutes. Some guys cried, some stared at the floor, others buried their heads. But no one moved a muscle until our captain, Chris Fragner, started taking his equipment off. Without it ever being spoken, that was everyone's cue.

When Fragner headed to the shower, he stopped, turned to his teammates, and finally spoke: "I just want to thank you taxi players for all the work you did for us this season. You guys were great."

Nothing else that night made me feel better.

We were utterly scrupulous about following the state and league rules, even the ones we knew other teams were breaking. But I did break one rule, and I would happily break it again. State rules said that as soon as your season ended you couldn't practice anymore. But we'd already rented the ice, and it wasn't cheap. So when the players asked if they could skate the rest of the week, I said sure. We weren't trying to get any competitive advantage. They just wanted to have fun and enjoy each other's company for a few more days — all of which helped get the bad taste out of our mouths.

Almost all the players and coaches chose to come down to our rink after school to play some pickup hockey games. They weren't sick of hockey, and they weren't sick of each other. They really didn't want the season to stop, the team to disband, and the experience to end.

All those feelings were on full display two weeks later at our senior banquet. I started by providing a brief overview of the team's accomplishments.

"Your mission was to prove that Huron's rightful place is at the very top of high school hockey, without selling your souls to do it," I said. "So we lined up the toughest schedule any Huron hockey team has ever played to see what you were made of.

"In the off-season, day after day, for four months, you found your limits — and destroyed them. This inner knowledge, earned through heat waves and pouring rain and snow flurries when no one else was watching, became your secret weapon."

They had finished our third season together with a 17-4-5 record — Huron's fewest losses and best winning percentage, just three years after suffering a winless season. Their fourteen-game unbeaten streak set another school record and included Huron's first win over Pioneer in five years, and first ever victories over three different Metro League opponents.

In the Metro League, the River Rats won eight games — as many as the previous five years combined — and finished third out of twelve teams, three years after almost dropping out of the league. We played twenty-two different teams that season, lost to three, and outshot all of them but Trenton, in our second meeting. The River Rats were no longer scared of anyone.

In my banquet speech I reminded them of our very first meeting on Henry's back deck three years before. When I told them then that we'd be fighting for a state title, everyone thought I was crazy — with good reason. Three years later nobody thought that was crazy, including the state champions themselves, who'd been scouting us in the playoffs.

In the process, our ranking rose from dead-last in the state to a high of fourth, Huron's highest ranking in two decades, and fifty-third in the nation out of 993 teams — thereby passing 940 of the nation's teams, or 95 percent of the country.

On their team plaque posted in our locker room, the seniors decided to put:

2002–03:

17-4-5. BEST EVER.

It spoke for itself.

"These numbers tell an incredible story," I said at the banquet, "but as we often say, our numerical goals are just motivators to accomplish our true goals: work hard, support your teammates, and dream big. Your mission was to prove to the state that Huron hockey ranks among the very best, on and off the ice, and to prove to yourselves that nothing can shake the values you stand for. You have done all that and more.

"I will never forget you."

They were proud of their records, their big wins, their rankings, and their trophies, and rightly so — but those weren't the point. At the beginning of this book, I admitted I couldn't circle any numerical marks we needed to hit that would show that my vision of Huron hockey had come true. Likewise, three years later, I couldn't point to this statistic or that to prove we'd accomplished our mission either.

No, the proof came from the seniors' banquet speeches. They came prepared with notes, and spoke eloquently and emotionally about their experience. But they almost never mentioned any of their achievements.

Instead, they talked about the hard work everyone poured into our mission when no one was watching; they talked about defining themselves individually and as a team, including their goals; they talked about how good it felt to come to the locker room every day, and how it was the closest team they'd ever played on.

They saw themselves differently than they had just a few years before.

"Had our team won the state championship, or any other trophy, or game, I would not have walked away any better off," recalls Chris Fragner. (Despite his fears that playing for Huron would end his hockey career, Fragner would play three seasons for the University of Michigan's top-ranked team.) "In fact, I think that because we didn't reach the pinnacle of our season, all of us remained humble and carried on the lessons we learned from Coach Bacon. We didn't get distracted by winning to miss all the important stuff."

Yes, in the end the hockey gods had denied us what we had worked so hard to achieve, what we felt was our destiny. But it turned out that really wasn't the point, after all.

A bunch of individuals had come together to forge a tremendous team capable of doing extraordinary things. They were very proud of who they had become, and grateful to have been on the journey together.

I was too.

- One of the toughest tests any leader faces occurs immediately following a success or failure. If you take the credit or pass the blame, your people will never look at you the same way. But if you give away the credit and accept the blame, you'll foster more loyalty from the people you need the most.

- Remember: leaders get criticized. It's inevitable, so take it as a compliment and learn what lessons the criticism has to teach.

- Don't ever worry about getting enough credit. If your team succeeds, you will always get far more than you need. "The reward of a job well done is to have done it."

Epilogue:
Coach Lapper

Three months later, when we started our informal summer season in late June, Mike Lapprich, or Coach Lapper as everyone called him, was witnessing his world opening up. He was about to turn twenty-three, he had moved into his own place, he had just been admitted to nursing school, and he had even appeared in the pages of *Car & Driver* magazine, based in Ann Arbor, where he worked on the side.

But the highlight for him was the night he and his younger brother Kevin were on the same bench for our first summer league game, as coach and player. Kevin even tallied two assists in the contest, a promising debut.

After the game Lapper went back to his parents' house for dinner, and gushed about Kevin's play. For Lapper, life didn't get much better.

Early the next morning, June 25, 2003, I got a call from Lapper's mom. She told me Mike had been in a car accident the night before, and died instantly.

I was in disbelief. When I gathered the players later that day in our locker room to break the news, they were too. Lapper was their big brother, and for most of them the first person they were close to who had died. Their sobbing was uncontrollable.

So many people showed up for Lapper's funeral that the overflow crowd had to stand in the foyer. We named the Unsung Hero Award, a scholarship, and our locker room in Lapper's honor. Above the "atomic clock" we framed the picture capturing the emotional moment the year before when the players had given him the Unsung Hero Award.

But there was nothing we could do to lessen our loss.

Lapper's parents buried him in his green shirt and gold tie. At his grave site, in the shadows of Huron High and the VA Hospital, where Lapper had volunteered, the pastor said a few words. When he finished, I escorted Lapper's parents to their car, then walked back up the gentle slope.

I saw our players walking down in their trademark green shirts, but without their gold ties. *This is not how we do it,* I thought, and on this day of all days. But I decided they'd already been through enough, so I kept my comment to myself.

Then Chris Fragner, the '03 captain, and Stevie Wasik, who would be one of the '04 captains, walked up to me, red-eyed. Both put an arm around my shoulders. Fragner pinched the knot of my gold tie, and said, "Coach, we have a place for these."

The two then walked me up to the grave site. When we got there, I saw Lapper's casket draped with five dozen gold ties.

I lost it — for Lapper's passing, for our loss, and for my love for the young men who did that.

I learned later that while I had been walking Lapper's parents to their car, the players had stood around Lapper's casket, silent, at a complete loss. That's when Jon "Elmo" Eldredge decided to pull his "old gold" tie from his forest green shirt and lay it on Lapper's casket. Those ties meant a lot to those guys — "strong and bold in green and gold" — but of course, Lapper meant so much more.

"'Gold ties go with Lapp' kept ringing in my ears as we all sobbed together," Elmo recalls. "Loosening my tie, I felt like it was honoring the man who never asked for anything in return. It was saying goodbye to my friend, my carpool buddy, my motivator, Huron's north star. The gold ties didn't cost much and they weren't fancy, but they were a symbol of how far we had come."

Without a word, Elmo's teammates all followed his lead.

Lapper's legacy was not having his name on a locker room door or a trophy or a scholarship. It was helping dozens of boys become men — something they carry with them to this day.

It was never about the hockey.

Afterword

The next year was my last coaching the River Rats. We brought in Dave Debol, a University of Michigan All-American who had played with Gordie Howe and his sons in the NHL. He'd since coached Dexter's high school team to school records. We planned for Debol to take over Huron's team by himself the next year.

We had just graduated arguably Huron's best senior class, including four All-State players and our starting goalie. But as our fourth team's co-captain, Stevie Wasik, later explained to me, "It wasn't talent that built this team. It was leadership and culture."

Our fourth team didn't miss a beat, taking another Thanksgiving tournament trophy, another two-win sweep in the Michigan Hockey Showcase, and a win and a tie at Culver. The Rats were ranked in the top ten in the state throughout the season, which had become old hat for them.

The season's two biggest highlights included a win over undefeated, second-ranked Pioneer and our game one week later against defending state champion Trenton. Yes, the same team that had beaten us 13–2 my first year. But Trenton's banners no longer awed Huron's players, and their screaming fans had lost their power to intimidate.

The Rats fell behind 2–0, but we didn't panic. We controlled the play, outshot Trenton for two periods, and scored four unanswered goals to take a 4–2 lead into the third period. From there, our guys held on for a 4–3 victory, Huron's first over Trenton in two decades, and in more than forty tries.

After the final horn sounded, our players celebrated, but not as crazily as they had after our first win three years earlier, or after our first victory over Pioneer. This win was one to remember – but it wasn't considered shocking, or even an upset.

"When good teams play good teams," Trenton coach Mike Turner told their local paper, "you're going to win some and lose some."

A few weeks later Trenton would win its tenth state title.

"It's incredible," starting goalie Brian Commiskey told the *Ann Arbor News*. "They used to kill us. It's amazing how we did it [today]. I called up my brother, and he was crying."

When the game ended, I pulled our trainer, Rod Sorge, onto the ice to join the handshaking line. No one had suffered more losses in this building than he had, and I wanted him to enjoy it.

After our guys headed back to our locker room, Sorge looked at me, glassy-eyed, and said, "Come on."

I followed him through a side hallway to Trenton's older hockey rink, the site of more Huron drubbings than either of us could count. It was dark and silent except for the distant celebration we could hear going on back in our locker room.

"We stood quietly," Sorge recalls. "Nothing needed to be said. Times had indeed changed. That night a road trip left two men standing in an empty arena, alone in the dark, somehow smiling through their tears."

Acknowledgments

Every book I've written has its own personality, and this book has more personality than most — by design.

Obviously, without the Ann Arbor Huron High School River Rats hockey team, there wouldn't be a book. So, first and foremost, a heartfelt thank you to those who made coaching so fulfilling: my boss, athletic director Jane Bennett; Rod Sorge and Steve Sheldon, who drove the decision; the parents who gave so much; our first-class coaching staff; and of course the players, the heroes then and now. (All coaches and players are listed on pages 229–230.)

I know I've said it before, but it's worth repeating: I love you guys.

I started skating and playing as soon as I could, thanks to my parents, George and Grace Bacon. They drove me to rinks at five in the morning, replaced our garage door after my brother and I ruined the first one shooting pucks at it, and much to my surprise, when I started coaching, they came to almost every game, including the road trips. I'm so glad I could share this ride with them.

I had considered writing about coaching the Rats after my first season, which was pretty audacious since I hadn't yet published a single book. But even as I published other books about sports, business, and leadership, I could never figure out how to approach this subject until someone else figured it out for me. When I visited New York in October 2019 for a tour stop for my previous book, Larry Kirshbaum, a legend in publishing circles and a longtime friend, came down for the talk and joined me and a couple friends for pizza and a beer. He told me I needed to get back in touch with another publishing legend, Rick Wolff, who had edited Jack Welch's blockbuster *Straight from the Gut,* and five dozen other *New York Times* best-sellers.

When Rick asked if I had anything more in the leadership field, his specialty, I timidly mentioned my experience coaching the River Rats and sent him a TEDx talk I had given on the subject. I added that I had just created a new class at the University of Michigan, "Leading by Coaching," where my students had opened my eyes about what truly matters when we lead. (Thanks to them too.)

To my surprise, Wolff was intrigued and asked me to write up an overview and a couple sample chapters — then a couple more, and a couple more, until finally the folks at Houghton Mifflin Harcourt were convinced we had a book to write. Rick brought his vision and expertise to shape this book — which was not, he stressed repeatedly, to be just about high school hockey, but leading people in all manner of organizations. Rick cracked the code, and I'm immensely grateful for his faith, passion, and expertise — not to mention years of friendship.

I saw it as a very good sign when the publisher herself, the sharp, sensitive, and savvy Deb Brody, took this book under her wing, then assigned her A-Team to help, including attorney Loren Isenberg (who cried three times while reading it, God bless her), production editor Laura Brady, copyeditor Cindy Buck, interior designer Chloe Foster, jacket designer Mark Robinson, production coordinator Rita Cullen, publicist Megan Wilson, and marketing strategist Andrea DeWerd. They all took great care with a book I care a great deal about. Thank you!

Another big thank you goes to my agent at William Morris Endeavor, Jay Mandel, who has gamely guided a few of my unconventional proposals into good books with great publishers, including this one, with consummate skill and good humor. His assistant, Sian-Ashleigh Edwards, has been a treat to work with throughout.

The heroic efforts of the coaches and players not only made this experience worth writing about, they went above and beyond helping me write it, sending me some 150 pages of memories, ideas, and insights, and enduring countless calls. Their contributions, I believe, not only elevate the story, but separate this book from most leadership accounts. A big thanks to Huron coaches Jef Forward, Ned Glysson, Dale Rominski, Rod Sorge, and Pete Uher, and to Culver's Al Clark; plus almost half the players I coached: Steve Beltran, Larry Cattell, Bobby Chappuis, Pat Commiskey, Rob DeMuro, Adam Dwyer, Jon "Elmo" Eldredge, Chris Fragner, Ross Gimbel, Pete Heeringa, Mike Henry, Chris Kwon, Chris Kunkel, Scott "Scooter" McConnell, Dave McMurtrie, Tim Nowling, Mike Perry, Jake Ramsey, Nate Reichwage, Matt Rolen, Bobby Shahidehpour, Allan Sheldon, Dan Sheldon, Adam Was, and Stevie Wasik. Special thanks to former Chelsea Bulldog Josh Barron, who graciously confirmed the details from the famous fight. All-Star hockey parents Rob and Jill Chappuis, John Keedy, and Robin Kunkel also provided helpful accounts of those years.

The people above also read all or part of the manuscript, to make sure we got it right — no small assist. I also pulled in some business and hockey experts, including David Brophy, a professor at Michigan's Ross School of Business and former Ohio State hockey player; Todd "T.J." Johnson, hockey buddy and financial pro; Al "Doc" Loehr, a longtime Culver friend; John Lofy, trusted editor; David Harlock, a former Olympic and NHL player who's now a successful businessman; David Stringer, who played goalie at Amherst before becoming an unforgettable humanities teacher at Huron; and Peter Tomozawa, a former Huron captain and Goldman Sachs partner, now part-owner of the Vegas Golden Knights and Seattle Sounders, for which he also serves as vice president.

I have repeatedly relied on a trio of savvy readers: editor Thomas

Lebien; James Tobin, an acclaimed author and professor; and my wife Christie. They approach each manuscript from different perspectives, but they invariably provide invaluable insights and suggestions, giving me enough confidence to hit "send" on the final draft. Thank you.

I owe the greatest gratitude to Christie, the love of my life, and our son Teddy for their understanding, sacrifices, and good cheer while I was toiling in the "writer's cave." They even took trips together to give me more time and space to finish without going any crazier than necessary — to say nothing of the love we share. They are my best reasons for doing what I do.

This is the sixth book I've finished since we had Teddy, but the first one that Teddy was truly aware of while I was writing it, so his patience was particularly appreciated.

Daddy's done, little buddy. Now let's go play some hockey.

Ann Arbor Huron High School
River Rats Ice Hockey Team
Players and Coaches, 2000–2004

Players

Kevin Arabejo

Steve Beltran

Noah Bradley

Larry Cattell

Bobby Chappuis

Paul Choi

Pat Commiskey

Brian Commiskey

Phil Coron

John Davidson

Rob DeMuro

Adam Dwyer

Travis Dziubinski

Jon Eldredge

Keith Ferris

Chris Fragner

Ross Gimbel

Pete Heeringa

Mike Henry

Evan Julian

Ian Krell (manager)

Rob Keedy (manager)

Chris Kunkel

Chris Kwon

Kevin Lapprich

Steve Luongo

Ben Lutzeier

Jeff Marley

Brian Mastey

Scott McConnell

Dave McMurtrie

Perry Merillat

Mark Moran

June Naiki

Adam Novak

Tim Nowling

Mike Perry

Aaron Peterson

Peter Pritchett

Jake Ramsey

Nate Reichwage

Tom Renkes

Yaniv Ribon

John Riley

Matt Rolen

Kyle Ryder (manager)

Bryan Schultz

Brad Segall

Bobby Shahidehpour

Allan Sheldon

Dan Sheldon

Benjamin Silvers (manager)

Nick Standiford

Aki Suzuki

Shou Suzuki

Adam Was

Steve Wasik

Steve Yeum

Jerzy Zdrojkowski

Coaches

Rob Brown

Mike Chang

Jef Forward

Ned Glysson

Dave Griffith

Mike Lapprich

Ted Martens

Donnie O'Brien

Dale Rominski

Mike Schmidt

Rod Sorge

Bill Tucker

Pete Uher

Index